CHECKMATE LIFE

By

J. PRINCE

Copyright *Checkmate Life*

2021 J. Prince

All rights reserved

ISBN: 9798594649200

Printed in the United States of America.

What readers are saying ...

"Three words describe this book: impressive, amazing, and liberating!!!! I totally can connect with so many things you mentioned and experienced! Goosebumps all the way! Oh, my my! There is so much in the book that I took notes on." **Dr. CT**

"There is a lot of good stuff in here, plenty of valuable life lessons, and you've inspired in me the desire to dust off my old chess board. Might have to play tonight." **Amadeus**

"Reading your book was fun and often easy to read. As someone who is not familiar with chess, you allowed me to understand how life can imitate chess, as far as making the right or wrong moves, and other factors." **Wonder**

"I really enjoyed reading this mix of memoir and self-help book. You took a unique approach to teach life lessons with parallels to chess. As a reader that's only casually familiar with chess, I was still able to easily understand the lessons and metaphors." **Raven**

Thank you for allowing me to read your book. It is so interesting. I too have worked with at-risk youth and done gang intervention. I also understand some of the challenges youth in St. Louis face. I was there during the protests and participated in them as well. I was a teen mother at 14 and had many struggles in my life." **Cecilia Jones**

"Checkmate Life is true gift to anyone .I am truly inspired by your words. Your way of conveying the message to youth and the constant desire you have, to motivate them with your life experiences astonished me." **Ebony Thompson**

"The book is fantastic. I love how you incorporated chess and life. I think this book is very relatable, and anybody can benefit from reading it. I would not only recommend it to youth, but to anybody wanting to improve their lives." **Sabrina Ullcki**

"This book was excellent!! It was truly inspiring. Me as an experienced adult learned more from this book than what my parents taught me. It gave me excellent tips and ideas and ways I should follow when achieving my objective! I will definitely use them down the line of life!" **BP**

"Checkmate Life is a very inspiring book, well-detailed and written by a professional chess player with vast experience in the game and track records as a mentor to young people. The designs and graphic aids makes reading more explanatory, interesting and comprehensive." **EB**

"After thoroughly reading through this book, I must say that this book is the best life changing gift any young person can receive. You told your truth in the most open, motivating and liberating way. I believe that anyone who reads this book will be so inspired and motivated by your story and they will make the decision to break free from the chains created by fear, failures, disappointments, ignorance, pain and walk into the light of who they were truly created to be." **VC**

"You did an amazing job with the book! The way you brilliantly likened life to a game of chess and used it to teach your audience the core values of life such as discipline, humility, gratitude, perseverance and how they can apply these values to their everyday lives is mind blowing. Your ability to simplify deep lessons that would have been otherwise complicated for your audience is profound." **KM**

DEDICATION

To all the young people that are dealing with trauma,

there is a light at the end of the tunnel.

Just hold on. Don't give up.

You may be detoured, but don't be deterred.

"Life is Chess,

Chess is Life"

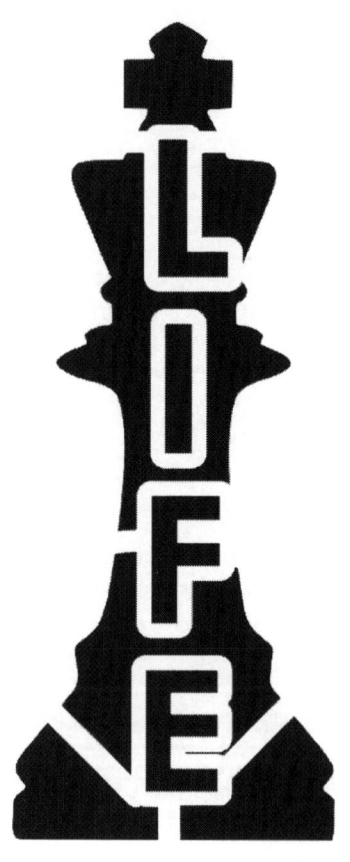

Contents

Calculate the Rules....... 25

Harmonize................. 46

Establish a Plan........... 63

Consistency............... 79

Key Players............... 94

Maintain Vigilance......... 112

Actionize Opportunities 127

Tune-Up 154

Enlighten Others.... 177

About the Author

The only person you are destined to become is the person you decide to be.

~

Ralph Waldo Emerson

I know this is going to sound unbelievable, but what I am about to tell you is 100 percent true. My grandmother's birth name was Queen. My grandfather's birth name was King. My mother's birth name is Princess. And my birth name is Prince. Names are important because they play a part in shaping your identity. With the name Prince I was destined to be a leader. Unfortunately, I have not always lived up to that name. It has been a long journey. I have fallen short and continue to do so, but I keep striving, I keep getting up. There was a time in my adolescence when I wasn't sure I'd make it to eighteen.

You see, my upbringing left me lost and adrift, as I had very little guidance from an early age. The home I grew up in was dysfunctional and full of mental, physical, and substance abuse. With no good examples to follow and nobody to keep me on the right path, I began to fight and commit crimes as ways to channel all my emotions. My schooling suffered, I failed the seventh grade, and was expelled on two separate occasions. I was in a constant state of rage. I needed help.

When I was fourteen years old, help came in the form of my 5'3" grandmother Queen, nicknamed Big Momma. She brought me in when I was at my lowest and changed the trajectory of my life forever. The funny thing about being lost is that you don't even know you are lost. Big Momma gave me unconditional love despite all that I had done and gave me hope that I could be a benefit to society instead of a detriment.

Big Momma helped me emotionally, but academics were another matter. I was still without a spark and primarily made Cs and Ds. I felt like

people who did homework were suckers. I didn't see a reason to excel in school; I had no intention of going to college and barely made it out of high school. With no real direction, I joined the Army. I thought that way, at least I could get paid and have three meals a day. I had no idea what being a soldier truly meant.

Being a soldier means waking up at 5:00 a.m. every day. Being a soldier means digging foxholes in the hardest ground imaginable in extreme heat in the desert. Being a soldier means putting your life on the line every day for strangers.

I made a promise to God that if he allowed me to make it out of the service alive, I would dedicate myself to school. He kept his end of the bargain, so I had to keep mine. When my three years of active military service ended, I enrolled at Western Illinois University. My first semester, I received all As and thus had a 4.0 GPA.

Amazing what the fear of losing your life will do for you.

I graduated with a BA in psychology and a 3.4 cumulative GPA, then matriculated into Southern Illinois School of Law. The journey didn't get any easier. Three times I took the bar exam after law school, and three times I failed. It was utterly demoralizing. I didn't know what I was going to do with the rest of my life. I was lost and confused again.

I started substitute teaching as a way to make ends meet, and I discovered my calling in helping young people. It's so amazing that through our failures, our true destiny can be illuminated. I started sharing my story and began connecting with young people. One of the things I started sharing was how to play chess.

I find it ironic that the only thing my abusive stepfather gave me other than trauma, was an introduction to chess. He taught me the game, and I've used it to open up many doors and opportunities. Troubled adolescents tend to have a view that there are no options other than the

miserable hand dealt to them. Let me tell you, they are wrong. The world is truly their oyster.

The biggest irony of my story is that it was a troubled teen who properly taught me chess: a seventeen-year-old prodigy named KG. While I had a basic understanding of the game from my stepfather, I lacked a deep understanding. The things KG knew were astounding, and I began to understand I really knew nothing about chess.

But KG was as challenged by life as he was great at chess. He was caught in drinking and drug addictions. His mother died when he was young, he had a poor relationship with his father, and he had tried to take his own life. Despite it all, KG broke the game down before my eyes, and in turn I tried to mentor him through life. As this went on, I began drawing parallels between the games of life and chess, which caused me to reflect on some of my previous failures in life.

As I reflected, my failure in law school came from attempting to memorize everything and lacking the ability to apply the information in my head. It

occurred to me that many of the youths I was teaching were just like me; they struggled to take in new information and apply it to their everyday lives. They were almost there, and I felt called to help them make that leap.

After that, I began teaching chess with a better understanding of the game and related it to life stories, parables, and quotes. As I spent more time with these young people, I saw them retain more information and apply it to their lives. That's when I knew I was on to something.

It's my ultimate goal to give back to the community. I've experienced the consequences of a dysfunctional upbringing and know the importance of a mentor figure in the lives of troubled youth. Now I am a husband, father of four, college graduate, chess instructor, mentor, and aspiring author. I feel it is my duty and obligation to help those in similar circumstances, and like ripples from a pebble in a pond, I need to reach out. I have dedicated my life to helping at-risk youth, working with the Department of Social Services, Family

Court, the St. Louis Public School System, the St. Louis Chess Club, and the Kappa Alpha Psi Fraternity Incorporated mentoring program.

Instead of "reach one teach one", I want to teach millions. What better way to do so than a book and curriculum?

YOUNG LIVES MATTER

Acknowledgments

How does a person say *thank you* when there are so many people to thank? This book is a thank you to my grandmother, who taught me love and compassion. The people most responsible for this book becoming a reality are all the young people I have mentored and taught. You all motivated me to practice what I preached and to leave the world in a better place than I found it.

Introduction

Change your thoughts and change your world.

~

Norman Vincent Peale

I had three friends: a young one, a rich one, and a lost one who didn't know where he was going in life. The young one was a highly accomplished chess prodigy, a national master with a rating of more than 2200 out of 2700. He didn't have a penny to his name, he was just starting college and trying to find himself.

The rich friend was a millionaire who knew very little about chess. He was a husband and father of two, and a former NFL star with a thriving construction business.

The third friend was me.

You, yourself, as much as anyone in the entire universe, deserve your love and affection. ~Buddha

I was not applying myself at all. I was not very good at chess—or life: I had two degrees, a dead-end job, a failed marriage, a dysfunctional relationship with my four children, and no bank account. I was overweight, drove a 2004 Ford Taurus in 2020, and slept on my cousin's couch.

One day, I heard a talk by the famous motivational speaker Myles Monroe about renewing your mind. He told a story about how even though the elephant is the biggest and strongest animal, when he sees a lion, he is scared and sees himself as lunch. When the lion sees the elephant, he sees the elephant as lunch too. It's not the physical attributes; it's the mindset. Your attitude is defined by your belief system.

That's when I thought to myself: *I'm tired of being lunch.* I was too smart and talented to lead such an unfulfilled life. I began researching, watching more videos, and learning from the most successful people closest to me.

I began to consult both friends about their strengths so I could be better myself. I have always wanted to be a great chess player—maybe it was a way of defeating my abusive stepfather (who was the first to introduce me to the game)—and being successful in life. As I was processing the information, I started realizing both friends were saying similar things but using different terminology. I wondered: *How can the rich friend be bad at chess and the young friend be equally as bad at life?*

So my psychology degree kicked in. I realized neither friend was using associative learning, which is when ideas and experiences reinforce each other and can be mentally linked to one another. In a nutshell it means our brains were not designed to recall information in isolation; instead, we group information into one associative memory. That's why it's difficult to recall just one eyebrow from an isolated picture without seeing the whole face. In conclusion, my two friends were not associating their knowledge of the thing they were good at with the

thing they were bad at. They didn't see the similarities.

Around that time, I began teaching chess to beginner players, focusing on the names of the pieces, how they move, and all the basics. I found there was a point where the players stopped learning as much, and their interest in the game faded. I started using the associative learning method in hopes it would inject some enthusiasm. It worked! The kids started retaining more information, and some of them even started beating me. Maybe it worked too well.

This process opened my eyes as well. Reading chess books, watching videos on self-improvement, and taking chess lessons from my young friend, I started to see more similarities. They all used comparable principles, talking about beliefs, vision, opportunities, planning, and so on. That's when I had that *ah-ha* moment. I slowly incorporated these associative principles into my everyday life and chess, and to win at both, I began approaching life as a chess match.

I started with a vision of where I wanted to see myself, setting realistic objectives and goals. This helped me gradually lose weight, and I didn't just get a new job; I got three (Chess Instructor, Programs Specialist, and Student Discipline Coordinator). I worked on my marriage, started addressing my parental issues, and finally earned enough money to purchase a new car and move back with my family.

I even wrote this book, which details that journey, what I learned, and how these principles helped me have a fulfilled and effective life. In part, I hope it becomes your journey too.

This is a roadmap to success, to escape a bad situation, to a better life. I illustrate my points with stories, information, acronyms, quotes, and so much more to help make the lessons memorable. You will be able to *Checkmate Life* and your opponent simultaneously.

Chapter 1 starts by calculating the rules of the game. If you don't know the rules, it makes it impossible to win. How will you know if you won? In Chapter 2, you'll discover why you must be in

harmony and accord with yourself; because otherwise, your purpose and goals will never be fully materialized. If you are not in harmony, you will work against yourself and not reach your destination in a timely and efficient manner. Time is your most valuable resource. There is no time pill that gives you more of it. Every second must be maximized.

After shifting mindsets regarding the rules of the game and your true opponent, you can establish a plan in Chapter 3. You will do this by recognizing you can connect your approach to life with your strengths, hopes, and goals.

Setting **s**pecific, **m**easurable, **a**chievable, **r**elevant, and **t**imely (SMART) goals are key, as are balancing your goals against your strengths and weaknesses and recognizing your opportunities and threats when striving for these goals.

Once the importance of goal setting and the strategy in defining goals is established, Chapter 4 will explore the importance of consistently working on your goals and sticking to your plan. I discuss distractions as well as habits, and will help you

recognize that knowledge leads to feelings that lead to actions, which consequently leads to your current situation. You therefore must control what information you allow into your brain.

It's important to recognize that while you might sometimes take a detour from your goals, you don't need to be deterred from them because of adversity. Don't give up. Restarting is just as valid as starting. I'll dive into beliefs, as well. Rather than going through the motions, you need to believe in your future and your goals in order to stick to your plan.

Chapter 5 will discuss the importance of relevant resources—support or assistance that is directly related to the issue at hand, that can be verified, and is accurate. This can be family, friends, co-workers, mentors, books, the Internet, and even yourself. As with the game of chess, you'll need multiple pieces to win, all of which complement each other in different ways. You must know the strengths and weaknesses of these pieces, and they must work in unison, strategically.

In Chapter 6, you'll learn to maintain vigilance. Once you're on course, you need to remain dedicated to your destination. Also, maximize your potential by incorporating constructive criticism; as well as positive feedback, regardless of the source. And as with chess, you must notice and account for the opposition's movements.

Chapter 7 will help actionize your opportunities. After executing your plan and coordinating with your resources, you must learn how to seize opportunities—without being too passive or too aggressive— so you can achieve your goals.

Chapter 8 is a reminder that everyone needs a tune-up. You need to maintain proficiency and sharpen your skills in everything you do. The journey is not complete when you reach your goal because you'll set new goals and objectives. You should always strive to achieve more in every human endeavor.

Chapter 9 is about striving to reach full potential, which can only happen by helping others. We were all created to serve others. We are who we help. True

success is measured by how many people we have helped. This is especially true for our children, as they are our greatest asset. They are our future.

Youth advocate Josh Shipp says it best: "Every kid is one caring ... [person] away from being a success story. Their genius is many times camouflaged as an annoyance. We just have to redirect the annoyances and cultivate the talent."

The *we* can be anyone. Every man, woman, or child can be a mentor and help others. There is only one quality necessary to be a mentor—just care.

Chapter 1

Calculate the Rules of the Game

How dreadful ... to be caught up in a game and have no idea of the rules.

~
Caroline Stevermer

What Are Rules and Why Do We Need Them?

Rules are necessary for us to live and function in all phases of our life. Rules set boundaries, limits, expectations, and consequences. Rules control anything you can think of. Rules control your school, your home, your family, your job, the movie theatre, driving, and even restaurants. Chess and life are no different. If you want to be successful at either or both, you must first learn the rules.

In this chapter, I'll cover the types of rules that exist, their importance, and the connection between them in life and chess. If you want to learn the basic chess rules or you encounter chess related words in this book that you do not understand please review my other book, *Chess Basics*.

Something to Think About

What if everyone could simply get up and do whatever they wanted to during class? Do you think much learning would take place? Instead of an orderly, peaceful learning environment, a classroom without rules would be pure chaos. Would you like to be in that environment? Could you learn in it?

What if the world was based on the survival of the strongest? Whoever was bigger or stronger would just take everyone else's things. Instead of enjoying video games, working, going to the mall, or going to the park, every day would be like the *The Purge*. Would you like to be in that environment? Could you survive in that environment, and if so, for how long? Could your parents, brothers, sisters, and grandparents survive in that world?

What would happen if you were playing chess or any other game with no rules? There would be chaos. Players would be fighting each other. The game would be too competitive, with no referees to stop unsportsmanlike behavior. If there were no rules, how would you win? Would it even be fun playing?

Types of Rules

There are several types of rules to include: procedural, legal, scientific, religious, group/organization, self, and principles. It may seem overwhelming at the start; there are so many rules. The good news is that there are differences between them, but there is a lot of overlap between them as well.

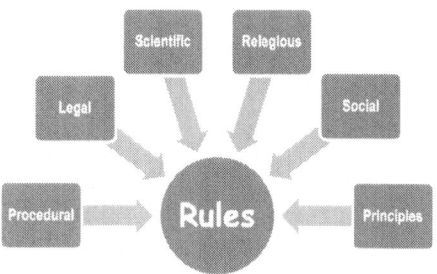

(1) Procedural

Procedures are specific sets of steps to follow when performing tasks. Those tasks can be how to play chess, entering the classroom, going to the restroom, requesting a pencil, asking a question during a class discussion, handling conflict, etc. Procedures allow you to set the same expectations for every person involved.

(2) Legal

Laws are rules that bind all people living in a community. Laws protect our general safety and ensure our rights as citizens against abuses by other people, organizations, and the government itself. For young people to be successful and view themselves as valuable members of society, they must be equipped with legal knowledge and civic skills as well as the confidence to use these laws. Learning about

legalities can be a crucial component of work-training programs, and any life skills that provide teens with the tools they need to navigate in the adult legal world is an important step forward in the development of involved, committed, and competent young adults who can face the challenges of the future.

(3) Scientific

Science rules can show you that some rules may not be broken in our world. These rules are constants and do not take into consideration name, wealth, or ethnicity. They are what they are. There can be grave consequences for attempting to break them. An example of this is gravity, the force that attracts a body toward the center of the Earth. If you jump off a tall building without a parachute, you will suffer severe bodily consequences.

(4) Religious

Religion is a set of beliefs and rules held by a group of people. There are many different religions, each with different convictions about the world and its inhabitants, how it came about, and what its purpose is. These beliefs are often linked to supernatural beings, such as gods or spirits. They can also be connected to a concept, such as the direction that each person's spirit should take towards goodness, honesty, and duty; this is called spirituality.

Each religion also has a moral code, rules that govern how the followers should act. These types of rules include things like the Ten Commandments, which cover things such as not killing, lying, or stealing.

(5) Group/Organization/Community

Social rules are the set or pattern of behaviors expected to be followed by everyone as a member of a group. These rules are both written and unwritten. Some examples are, if you bump into someone, you usually say *excuse me,* or *I'm sorry*, and when someone is speaking, you don't cut them off to say something.

(6) Self

Self-discipline or self-control is the ability to avoid unhealthy decisions about anything that could lead to negative consequences. If you set rules for yourself, you often forgo instant and immediate gratification and pleasure in favor of some greater

gain or more satisfying results, even if it requires effort and time. It also speaks to what you will or won't allow in your life. These are your boundaries. You have to set these because no one knows you better than yourself.

(7) Principles

Most rules are situation-specific. They could require you to memorize a bunch of things or carry a manual around with you. On the other hand, principles alleviate the need for a multitude of rules. Principles are internalized, thoughtfully applied rules that can be used in countless situations. They can simplify our lives. Principles are a guide.

To checkmate life and chess, you must follow principles. A principle is a by-product, not a pursuit. Principles will protect, sustain, preserve, guard, and promote you.

Below are principles that are applicable in both life and in chess. I put them in the acronym STRIVER, so it will be easier for you to remember them.

Stay humble.

Time is our greatest resource, don't waste it.

Respect everyone.

In thyself believe.

Visualize success.

Every day get better.

Review before and after making decisions.

Stay Humble

Humility is genuine gratitude and a lack of arrogance, a modest view of one's self. It's not getting too down about mistakes or too happy about wins. It is staying emotionally even. There is always going to be someone better, faster, and stronger. After all, you didn't get to where you are in life without some assistance.

These realizations will allow you to grow. If you think you are superior to others, you will likely not work hard and try to improve as much as you possibly could. If you feel you are superior, you will likely not have good sportsmanship. If you think you are superior, you are likely to miss important details—this is especially true in chess and life.

One slip of attention can alter your life or game. One slip of attention can mean you miss an opportunity.

Nothing is more expensive than a missed opportunity.

Time is Our Greatest Resource

This moment in time will never come again. We need to appreciate every moment that we have and never waste time, as it waits for no one. You can't stop the clock or slow things down; it's going to keep going whether you want it to or not.

You must ensure that you do what you can to take every opportunity to make the most of your time. Die on the empty one; give it all you've got. Enjoy every single moment. Make every second count.

There are 86,400 seconds in a day. *What are you going to do with your time?*

Respect Everyone

Respect is the sense of worth or personal value that you have for others. You should acknowledge and appreciate that it's ok for others to have opposing opinions, views, ideas, abilities, perspectives, and knowledge. When you respect others, you'll find yourself listening more and talking less, and you may even reevaluate your perspectives. When you respect others, they tend to respect you back, which also leads to empathy, the ability to emotionally understand what other people feel, see things from their point of view, and imagine yourself in their shoes. It also minimizes confusion. When you don't respect your opponent, you often underestimate them. In chess and life, this can lead to defeat.

In Thyself Believe

Believing in yourself affects everything you do, from your professional life to your personal life, in your relationship with yourself and your relationships with others. It also affects the choices you make and the dreams you dream. How you view yourself, how you measure your value, how you assess your potential, and how you determine your worth will all combine to create the life you'll live.

From your days as a student on, the choices you make are determined by your belief in yourself. You choose your classes, your major, your training, your first job, and your military branch, not just based on what you think you might enjoy but based on what you think you are capable of and even deserve. Others like parents, guidance counselors, friends, and neighbors may have influenced your belief in yourself

by the judgment and advice they gave—good, bad, or otherwise—by thinking certain schools are long shots or safeties based on their perception of your ability, by telling you which job you were qualified for or had enough experience in. Sometimes these messages can be verbal with words like: *That's a really hard school to get into* or *Only the top students are ever chosen for that program.*

It all starts with your mindset, the conversations you have with yourself, and the messages you choose to believe. You can tell yourself that you're simply not good at something, or you can tell yourself that you can get better at anything you dedicate your energy to. You can talk yourself out of applying for a job you want because you think you'll never get it, or you can prepare a powerful cover letter. You can tell yourself you'll never be good at chess, or you can tell yourself you'll be a grandmaster.

Your reality is the reflection of your strongest belief. It's all up to you!

Visualize Success

Visualization is the art of seeing what is invisible to others. It is the mental picture of the future you desire. In other words it is the expression of your hopes and dreams. Having a vision means you have a clear sense of purpose. It means you have a bigger picture of your life.

Vision inspires action. A powerful vision pulls in all your resources. It creates energy and the will to make change happen. It inspires individuals to commit, to persist, and to give maximum effort. A vision allows you to create plans, goals, and objectives.

Suppose you don't know where you are going. How will you know if you've arrived? When I teach chess, one of my first lessons is: What does checkmate look like?

Every Day Get Better

Once you make the decision to improve, yesterday doesn't matter. You can be great starting today. Improving your life or chess game does not have to be about making one drastic change. Yard by yard is very hard, but inch by inch is a cinch. The hardest step is the first step. Just start!

Review Before & After Making Decisions

We are all human and make mistakes. As Wyatt Earp once said, "Fast is fine, but accuracy is everything." Another famous quote that goes with this principle is, "Measure twice, cut once."

If, and when, you make mistakes, learn from them. Make sure you don't make the same mistake twice.

What Happens If You Break the Rules?

If you break the rules, the rules may break you.

When I was in law school, there was a rule where students could only miss eight days of class before being dropped from the class itself. If you are dropped, you do not get credit for the class nor can take the final. At the time, I didn't agree with this rule. I thought if I was paying for tuition, then how could the teacher tell me how many days I could miss? As long as I passed the test, it should be up to me.

By the time there was only one week left in school before finals and graduation, I had already

missed the maximum number of days. I woke up late and missed the class because I overslept due to my overnight job. When I got to class the following day, the instructor pulled me out and told me I was being dropped because I had missed too many days. One of the other students had kept up with my absences and informed him. He apologized, but rules are rules. This meant I wouldn't be able to graduate because I wouldn't have enough credits.

It was devastating. I had a lot of family members coming in. What was I going to tell everyone? It was so embarrassing. What was I going to do?

I talked to the dean, and he told me they would let me walk, but I would have to come back and make up that credit in summer school, which I did and graduated. While that was a tough lesson to learn, it was very valuable for my growth. I learned there could be harsh penalties for breaking the rules, whether I agreed with them or not.

I violated a chess rule in my first chess tournament, and paid the price. I was forty years of age, and my opponent was nine. This is one of the

things I love about chess: anyone can beat anyone. Age, gender, ethnicity, or religious beliefs don't matter. Anyone can truly beat anyone.

The game was winding down, and I was in a winning position. All I had to do was checkmate him and not do anything dumb. Well, if I'm telling this story, it means I did something dumb. I attempted to move my knight, but after close consideration I decided against it. Unfortunately, I had already touched the knight. My nine-year-old opponent raised his hand to get the attention of the tournament director, who asked me if I touched the piece. I said yes. He told me I had to move the piece. Moving that knight meant that game was going to be a draw. I was devastated, but once again rules are rules.

I learned from that situation, and it's never happened again. I subscribe to the notion that it's ok to make mistakes, just not the same one repeatedly.

- Rules are necessary.
- Familiarize yourself with the rules before starting any endeavor.
- Use the rules/principles from the acronym STRIVER as your guide in chess and life.
- If you break rules, they may break you.
- Don't blame others for the negative consequences from a rule you break.

Chapter 2

Harmonize: Acknowledge the True Opponent Within

Happiness is when what you think, what you say, and what you do are in harmony.

~
Mahatma Gandhi

In the previous chapter, you learned that you must first learn the rules before undertaking any endeavor. Like in the game of chess, you now know how to move the pieces in your life., but you still don't know how to checkmate your opponent or life. What's next? You must now learn the purpose of each piece, the game, and your life.

The great Mark Twain said: "The two most important days in your life are the day you are born, and the day you find out why." Your why is your purpose. What were you born to do? What do you want to commit your life to? Success is measured by the fulfillment of your purpose, not against the success of others.

Not fulfilling your purpose can result in wasting time and energy. As I've mentioned before, time is our most valuable resource; we don't have it to waste. We do not know when our last moment will be. Therefore, every moment we waste could lead to incomplete fulfillment of purpose or mission. Our every action needs to be consistent with our purpose. If not, we are working against ourselves and are threatened with failure to complete our mission and thwart our purpose. This is called disharmony.

Our purpose and actions must match. This is called being in harmony. Webster defines harmony as being in agreement or accord. One must be in agreement or accord with oneself; if not, your purpose will never fully materialize. You will work against yourself and never get to your true destination. You will not complete your mission.

Have you ever been confused? Don't know how to start? Don't know what to do next? It seems like every decision you make is getting you in more trouble and making the situation worse.

Have you looked at your chessboard and not known what to move first? Have you ever played chess and your pieces are everywhere with no sense of direction or purpose? These situations represent disharmony. We are designed to have a purpose. Our chess pieces are designed to do certain things; they

have a purpose. When you have things out of order, it is expedient to get back in harmony.

As another example, a car is created as a means of transportation. When used for its intended purpose, it gets kids to soccer practice, parents to work, provides race car drivers and taxi drivers a living, and so on. If the car is used as something to sit on in your driveway and is not maintained, it will rust and wither away. The car will not achieve its purpose nor reach its destination. If a car could talk, it would say: "Get off me and drive me. I don't want to be wasted!"

Your purpose and destiny or destination should support each other. Your destiny is dependent on how well you fulfill your purpose. If you do things against your purpose, then your destination will be up to chance.

Let's look at another analogy: A hammer's purpose is to assist carpenters, hit nails, and pull out nails during the construction, building, or demolition process. Its proper destination is in a carpenter's or

builder's hands. The purpose and the destination align. If a person uses the hammer for an unintended purpose, the destination is not guaranteed. For example, if a person used a hammer as a weapon instead of its intended purpose, where might the hammer end up? It could end up in a police station's evidence room. It could end up in the trash or a lake because the misuser is trying to hide the evidence. The hammer could still end up in a carpenter's hand. Who knows? What we do know is if it is used for its intended purpose, the destination is more certain.

How Does This Relate to Life?

We all have a purpose. We have a reason to exist, reasons which have intended results. If you are intended to be a father or mother, your destination may be to live in a five-bedroom home with two kids.

In order for that to happen, your actions must be consistent with fulfilling your purpose and ultimately ending up in your destination. If you are committing crimes, your destination is more likely to be confinement. You could still end up being a father or mother living in a five-bedroom home, but it is unlikely. And if you did, it may not be with the spouse or home you were intended to have.

How Does This Relate to Chess?

When you're playing chess, you have a purpose. Let's say your purpose is to improve at chess. Your actions should match. Here are some matching actions: studying the rules, learning more about the game, learning from your mistakes, taking notes, asking questions, and playing people who are better, worse, and equal to yourself. You would be in

harmony when your actions match your purpose. What would disharmony—actions not matching your purpose—look like? Not learning the rules, only playing players you are better than, not learning from your mistakes, not taking notes, or not asking questions.

If You Have Made Mistakes and Don't Know Your Purpose, Is It Too Late?

No! As long as you're breathing, it's not too late to harmonize and find your purpose. Purpose is permanent and never changes, just like a car is still a car. You can start today. It doesn't matter what you have, or have not, done up to this point. Your mistakes and shortcomings can catapult you into your purpose and destiny. That car can be restored. You can be restored.

Don't forget the STRIVER principles from chapter 1. You should use them in conjunction with all things in this book. **S**tay humble. **T**ime is our greatest resource. **R**espect everyone. **I**n thyself believe. **V**isualize success. **E**very day get better. **R**eview before and after making decisions.

How Do You Find Your Purpose In Life?

Your purpose is in you; hence, you must look within. A tree is concealed in a seed; an apple tree comes from an apple seed. You have greatness in you; you may just not know it yet. What lies in you is greater than what is ahead of you.

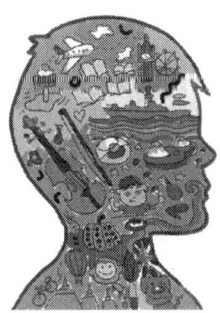

Look for obvious talents. Can you run fast or for long distances? Do you have a great voice? Do you have a great memory? Is math easy for you? Do you make friends easily? Can you draw? These are all examples of obvious talents. Once you find them, refine them. Invest in yourself. Become rare. Specialize. Refine yourself. Be unique. Then, you will be valuable.

The thing about talents is that they in themselves may not be your purpose. They can be gifts that help you achieve your purpose.

Have you ever heard of James Bond? If not, he's a fictional British secret agent. During his movies, he gets gifts or tools that help him accomplish his missions. He may get an exploding pen, a car that has a turbo boost, or eyeglasses with X-ray vision. These gifts are not his purpose, but they are things that help him on his mission or purpose. You may be comedic, but that doesn't mean you should be a comedian. You could be a teacher, doctor, salesman, or even a minister that uses comedy as an ice breaker.

Explore your interests. What do you like to do? I'm referring to things that are not burdensome when you do them; things you love to do and come easy to you. Listen to your inner compass. Are you enjoying what you do? Do you feel fulfilled? Can you read for hours? Do you like cleaning? Do you like helping people?

Try to narrow your interests down and combine them if you can. For instance, I like helping young people who have gone through or are going through traumatic experiences. I like playing chess. I also like teaching. I combined them, and now I'm a chess instructor for at-risk youths.

Read widely and endlessly. Learn and get ideas from others. This will open up possibilities that you didn't even know existed.

Don't do things you know are wrong or are likely to end poorly or violate the STRIVER principle.

Just try it! Don't be scared to try things. Steve Harvey says, "If you want to be successful, you have to jump. There's no way around it."

If it doesn't work, that's ok. Just take it off your list of things to try. Don't live with regret. No shoulda, coulda, woulda.

How Does This Relate to Chess?

The ultimate purpose in chess is trapping the king—checkmate. Each side has different chess pieces with different abilities to help or prevent checkmating the king.

Discover the attributes of each piece. Get better at using them. Specialize in using them. These gifts can help your purpose of protecting your king or trapping your opponent's king.

Find openings and defenses you enjoy playing.

Read widely and endlessly. Learn and get ideas from others. This opens up possibilities that you didn't even know existed.

Don't do things you know are wrong or likely to end poorly or violate the STRIVER principle.

Just play! Don't be scared to lose. You can't lose. You win every time you play, no matter the result. You will learn something as long as long as you gave it your all.

- [x] Success is measured by the fulfillment of your purpose.
- [x] When your purpose and actions match, you are in harmony.
- [x] When your purpose and actions don't match, you are in disharmony.
- [x] To find your purpose: look for obvious talents, explore your interests, read widely and endlessly, don't do things that violate the STRIVER principle, and just try it!
- [x] To find the purpose of each chess piece: discover the attributes of each piece, find openings and defenses you enjoy playing, read widely and endlessly, don't do things that violate the STRIVER principle, and just play!

Chapter 3

Establish a Plan

Proper planning and preparation prevent poor performance.

~
Stephen Keague

Once you know your purpose, you must create a roadmap or a path to fulfill it. This road or path, whether in life or chess, is called a plan. **Planning is thinking before the action takes place**. It allows you to prepare for the future. A plan helps determine how you could and should deal with a situation you encountered in the past, are currently dealing with, or more likely than not will encounter in the future. When you plan you prepare for the future with anticipation instead of apprehension or dread. Life is

easier if you can deal with the worst-case scenarios. This involves logical thinking and rational decision making.

Not just any road or path will do. You want to use the most effective and efficient plan. The words effective and efficient both mean *capable of producing a result*, but there is an important difference. Effective means *producing a result that is wanted*, while efficient means *capable of producing desired results without wasting materials, time, or energy*. There must be a balance between the two if you are going to be successful.

If you only concentrate on being effective, you will not consider time and procrastinate looking for the perfect scenario. If you only concentrate on time, you may rush through things and half do them. The VGOST method is the most effective and efficient road or path to handle this dilemma.

V … Vision: defines the optimal desired future state.

G … Goal: a list of outcomes you'll need to achieve your purpose and vision.

O … Objective: a measurable step you take to achieve a goal.

S … Strategy: the approach you take to achieve a goal.

T … Tactics: Patterns, combinations, or tricks developed to drive and support the strategy and get closer to the objective and/or goal.

Vision

The first step in creating a plan is formulating a vision. If you don't know where you're going, how will you know if you've arrived? Vision is the ability to see things as they could be, not as they presently are. You have to use your imagination. Having vision allows you to design the life you want. It controls your power of choice. You are the author. It's your life's story. It's your game. If you want to have a great day or life, it's up to you. It's also up to you if you want to have a bad day or uninspiring life.

Vision gives you direction to your destination. It's the address you put into the GPS system. Once you know where you are going, you know what roads will and won't take you there. If you don't have a vision, you will live a very loose life and will accept any road. It'll be hard for you to refuse things. Anything will do. A person with a vision lives a narrow life because vision simplifies life. You know what you will or won't do. When you have a vision,

there is no stress. Stress comes from not knowing what to do. You will know what to do.

SWOT Analysis

If you want your vision to work and flourish, it must be reality-based. It must be genuine and feasible. To ensure genuineness you must start with a current situation or position analysis. You must look at your strengths, weaknesses, opportunities, and threats. This is called a SWOT analysis.

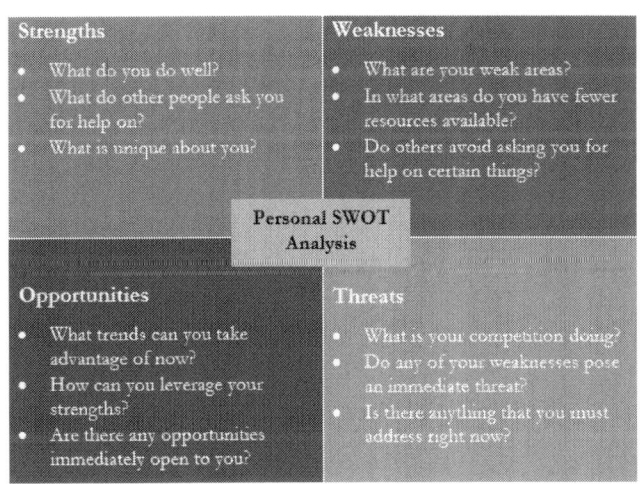

Personal SWOT Analysis

Strengths
- What do you do well?
- What do other people ask you for help on?
- What is unique about you?

Weaknesses
- What are your weak areas?
- In what areas do you have fewer resources available?
- Do others avoid asking you for help on certain things?

Opportunities
- What trends can you take advantage of now?
- How can you leverage your strengths?
- Are there any opportunities immediately open to you?

Threats
- What is your competition doing?
- Do any of your weaknesses pose an immediate threat?
- Is there anything that you must address right now?

Strengths	Weaknesses
• Hardworking • Openminded • Creative • Drawing	• Very busy • Indecisive • Impatient • Get bored quickly • Math
Opportunities	**Threats**
• Vacant position at work • Extra credit assignment • Open tryouts for the football team • Teacher's office hours	• Lose enthusiasm in project • Take too long to start on the project • Rush and put time over quality • Not complete by dead line • Failing course

Once you have done your SWOT analysis you must use that information for your GOST.

Goals

Once you have a vision, you must set goals to achieve that vision. Goal setting is simply making a list of things to do that will bring your vision into reality. Goals are the means to an end. A goal is something we strive for that should be aligned with our purpose, because reaching it will help us accomplish that purpose.

Well-designed goals are like magnets, they pull you in their direction. The harder you work on them, the harder the pull they will have on you. The best

thing about them, is that they can also pull you through some tough times. The best way to enjoy a meal is to get hungry. Once we reach a goal, be ready for the next one.

In conclusion, you should create well thought out and precise goals in order to be both effective and efficient. Another way of saying this is you must create S.M.A.R.T goals.

What Does S.M.A.R.T Mean?

SMART is an acronym that you can use to guide your goal setting. Your goals must be:

Specific: simple, sensible, clear.

Measurable: able to be tracked.

Achievable: realistic, attainable.

Relevant: must matter, at the right time, and be consistent with the plan.

Time bound: time based, meet deadline, have a reasonable end, timely, time-sensitive.

Example #1

I will get an A in math (specific) by studying an extra thirty minutes per day (measurable). During these thirty minutes, I will:

- review my notes from that day;
- read the related sections of the textbook; and
- write down any questions I have to ask my teacher (actionable).

It's important to me to reach a 3.5 GPA (relevant), so I can apply to the college of my choice. I will reach this goal by December 20 (time bound).

Example #2

I will earn $100 (specific) by July 10 (time bound). I will complete all my chores to earn my normal allowance. Also, I will work on five hours of extra projects every week (measurable). This will allow me to earn the money to enjoy going out with my friends (relevant). Every week I will (actionable):

- clean my room, do my laundry, and make sure all my stuff is put away;
- put dishes in the dishwasher, empty the dishwasher when it's done, and wipe down the kitchen counters;
- wash my mom's car and vacuum the inside;
- water the plants and clean up old leaves; and

- wash and clean the patio table.

Objectives

Objectives are detailed steps or stages that specifically identify how you will achieve a specific goal or goals. Therefore, your objectives must also be S.M.A.R.T.

Strategy

Simply put, strategy is your how. How will you achieve your goal and/or objective in a specific position or situation? How will you use your resources, skills, and knowledge collaboratively to solve a problem or find a solution that is hindering you from achieving your plan, vision, goal, and/or objective?

Example 1: The prom is in the next thirty days. I need $3,000, and I have no money. Assess current situation: SWOT analysis. Use VGOST. Vision: I envision myself in a sports car, wearing a tuxedo, with a beautiful date, and having fun at the after-party.

SMART goal: find legal ways to raise $3,000 in the next thirty days.

SMART Objectives: (1) Raise money without missing school, (2) don't want to borrow money, (3) don't want to commit any crime to get the money, and (4) raise it as quickly as possible because I have to order things and it may take some time.

Strategy: (1) Ask for an allowance, (2) ask for money that is owed to me, (3) do extra chores for money around the house, (4) start a GoFundMe account, and (5) pick up extra shifts on the weekend at work.

Note: each goal or objective can have its own strategy and tactic.

Example 2: Opponent is aggressively attacking my kingside.

Vision: You envision your king away from the pressure, on the other side of the board.

Assess current situation: SWOT analysis.

Use GOST Strategy: Try to castle queenside to relieve pressure. This is strategy because this may not be able to be done immediately. You may have to make a series of moves to make this happen. It is

going to require planning, setting goals and objectives.

Tactic: My bishop is preventing me from castling. I could trade my bishop for his knight, which will also put my opponent in check. He must take my bishop with his queen, which relieves some pressure and which also allows me to castle on the following move.

Tactics

Tactics primarily deal with observation and calculation. Tactics are patterns, combinations, or tricks developed to drive and support the strategy and get closer to the objective and/or goal.

Many tactics are timeless and have been used for centuries or even millennia. Military tactics such as ambushes, using prevailing weather, and divide-and-conquer have been around as long as people have fought each other. The same applies to tactics used by politicians and protesters.

Successful tactics often include an implementation intention, a specific trigger that signals when they should be used. Simply deciding

what to do is rarely enough. We need an *if this, then that* plan for where, when, and why. The short-term nature and flexibility of tactics allow us to pivot as needed. We should choose the right tactic for each situation to achieve our larger, strategic goals.

Example: Prom is the next thirty days, and I am broke and need to raise money.

Tactic: Monday is a holiday. I will work on Monday and get credit for sixteen hours instead of eight with no additional work. The only sacrifice is part of my holiday off day.

A chess tactic is a move, or a forced combination of moves, whereby you achieve a tangible objective. The goal of tactics is to forcefully advance your own position while simultaneously reducing the number of options your opponent has.

Analysis

There are things you should and should not do when you start a game. These are your opening principles. When you follow these principles, they turn into your roadmap or plan. I will list them below using the V-GOST method.

Purpose: win the game.

Vision: trap opponent's king.

Goal(s): follow opening principles.

Protect your King at all times.

Attack/Develop Toward the Center!

- Be effective and efficient in move selection
- Objective(s)

   Start the game with a central pawn move (queen or king pawn).

   Develop knights before bishops towards the center.

   Stay humble and respect your opponent during the game.

   Strategies; how will I stay humble and respectful?

- Every time my opponent moves, ask yourself what they are up to.
- Shake hands before and after the game.
- Don't talk and agitate your opponent.
- Don't move a piece twice in the opening, or at least your first eight to ten moves, unless forced to do so.
- Look for strengths and weaknesses in your position.

   Strategies; how will your pieces out fast?

• Look at each piece and ask yourself if it's protected and whether it can be taken before each move.

Can I be checkmated?

• Look for weaknesses and strength in your opponent's position before each move.

Strategies; how will you look for strengths and weaknesses?

• Look at each of your opponent's pieces and ask yourself is it protected and can it be taken

Can I checkmate my opponent?

• Get all of your pieces out as fast as possible, in the first eight to ten moves.

Strategies; how will your pieces get out fast?

Get Castled before Move Ten!

Be diligent in move selection.

Strategies; how will you be diligent?

• Before moving a piece, make sure it doesn't have a current job it is doing.

• Before moving, make sure the space you are moving to is safe (it won't be taken).

- Avoid exchanging a developed piece for an undeveloped counterpart if possible.
- Develop minor pieces before major pieces.
- Control more space than your opponent.
- Do not launch an attack before the development is completed.

Strategies; how will you make sure you don't attack too quickly?

Don't Bring Your Queen Out Too Early!
Tactic

Move pieces that satisfy more than one of the goals, if possible—aka best square.

- ☑ A plan is a roadmap or a path to fulfill your purpose.
- ☑ Your plan must be effective and efficient.
- ☑ The VGOST (vision, goal, objective, strategy, tactic) method allows you to be effective and efficient.
- ☑ The strengths, weaknesses, opportunities, and threats (SWOT) analysis ensures that your vision is achievable.
- ☑ Your goals and objectives must be SMART (**s**pecific, **m**easurable, **a**chievable, **r**elevant, and time-bound).
- ☑ Your strategy is how you achieve your goal and/or objective in a specific position or situation.
- ☑ Tactics are patterns, combinations, or tricks developed to drive and support the strategy and to get closer to the objective and/or goal.

Chapter 4

Consistently Stick to the Plan

Consistent hard work leads to success. Greatness will come.

~
Dwayne Johnson

After a while following these ideas, I had set goals and objectives, I was implementing strategies and tactics, but I was still not continuously winning at life and chess. Consequently, I made a list of things that were keeping me from succeeding. To my surprise, many of the items on this list were also weaknesses and threats from my SWOT analysis.

I thought to myself: *How can I let the same things beat me? I'm too smart for this!*

I was wasting energy and time on things that had nothing to do with my plan. I was allowing myself to be distracted.

Distractions break your concentration and draw your attention from your chosen interest, plans, goals, and objectives onto something else.

Imagine for example a basketball player who's attempting to shoot a free throw with the game on the line, while the opponent's fans are waving their hands to draw his attention from making the winning basket.

Just like the player, we cannot afford to be distracted; the game is on the line. Distractions can delay or prevent us from winning and succeeding in our destiny, mission, and purpose.

Let's be honest; we all struggle with distractions to some degree. Distractions can be grouped into two categories, internal and external. Internal distractions are thoughts and emotions generated by your self-image and perceptions. External distractions originate outside of you—auditory, visual, or physical. They are regarded as noise.

Internal Distractions

Winston Churchill had a perfect quote that deals with internal distractions: "When there is no enemy within, the enemies outside cannot hurt you."

You have to defeat your inner enemy first before taking on your real enemy. Defeat the things no one knows about. If you can control your thoughts, everything else is easy. The diagram below illustrates our thought process.

External Distractions

You must first figure out if it's really worth the fight or if it's a distraction. Put another way, is it real or just noise? If it's real, you must create a plan to implement strategies and utilize tactics to defeat them, as mentioned in the previous chapter.

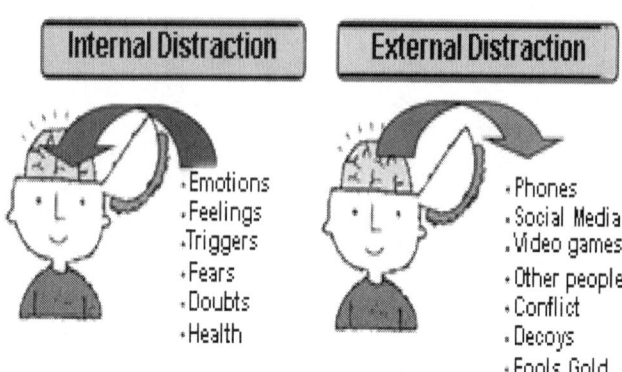

How Do You Eliminate Distractions?

The bad news is you cannot. You may eliminate a particular distraction, but there will always be others. The good news is you can minimize their effect on you. The key is to focus/concentrate your full attention and energy on something that's worth it.

Esther Hicks explains it best. "What you focus on grows."

That is the law of attraction. The law of attraction can be explained as *like attracts like*. This applies to our thoughts, words, and actions. Therefore, if you focus on distractions, they will grow. If you give your full attention to your plan, goals, and objectives, they will also grow, and you'll

have unlimited success. Below is a helpful acronym for focus.

How Do You Focus?

To improve your focus, you need to develop the skill of paying attention to a particular thought, task, or goal for a specified amount of time, without allowing distractions to break your concentration. This technique is similar to building muscles. You need to work on it a little bit every single day without fail, and your focus will improve. The resistance you overcome will hurt a little bit, but it will strengthen your willpower, and you will get a little stronger and more focused every day.

Full Attention On Chess And Life = Unlimited Success

Over time, the ability to focus deeply and for long stretches of time will be achieved.

Habits

The famous motivational speaker Jim Rohn once said, "Motivation is what gets you started; habit is what keeps you going."

Motivation is not reliable; it depends on your emotional state. And if you're not presently motivated, you can easily fall off the path. By picking up this book you have shown you are motivated to start on this road of change. If you want to stay on the road to fulfilling your purpose and achieving your goals and objectives, you will need to change your habits.

But what is a habit? A habit is a routine of behavior that is repeated regularly, and tends to occur subconsciously. The best way to change your bad habits is to replace them with new ones. When you create habits, your brain creates new neurological pathways, allowing you to use those habits more easily.

Robert Puller one said, "Good habits, once established, are just as hard to break as are bad habits."

In *The Power of Habit,* Charles Duhigg writes that our habits are responsible for most of what we do, which is best illustrated by the habit loop. In the loop our behavior is guided by cues, routines, and rewards. To change your behavior you need to isolate and identify the cues and rewards you're looking for.

The only thing you need to change is routine. For example, if you eat lunch at the same time every day, time is the trigger or cue, eating is the behavior—that's a habit. Enjoying the taste of the food is the reward. The more often the cue, behavior, and reward occur in close time and proximity to one another, the stronger a habit becomes.

This is true whether we're aware of it or not. Therefore, bad habits often can easily form if you're not careful.

Changing habits doesn't happen overnight. You must be patient and diligent. A study published in the *European Journal of Social Psychology* showed that the amount of time it took for a certain task to become

automatic—a habit—ranged from eighteen to 254 days. The average time was sixty-six days.

To create a new, healthy habit—or to break a bad one—you'll want to:

- determine the cue/trigger of the habit;
- determine the routine of the habit;
- identify the reward you are getting from the habit; and
- choose the desired behavior you want to replace, and choose what you want to replace it with.

Example 1

You want to create an after-school homework and chore routine.

1. Cue/trigger alarm clock that goes off at 4:00 p.m.
2. Start with completing your homework on the first day. That simple. Maybe add vacuuming the next day, then emptying the trash the day after that, and so on.
3. Your reward will be playing video games when you complete the task.

4. The behavior you want to replace is doing nothing.

5. Don't beat yourself up if you miss a day; do it the following day. The point is the process.

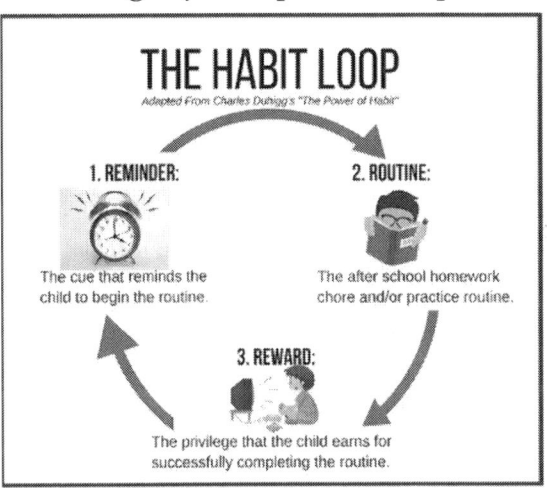

Example 2

You want to check if the opponent has any captures, checks, or threats.

1. Cue/trigger every time the opponent moves.

2. Start with captures. Are any of your pieces threatened to be taken? That simple. Then

maybe checks. Are you in check, or in danger of being checked? Then maybe threats. Are there any threats or pending threats?

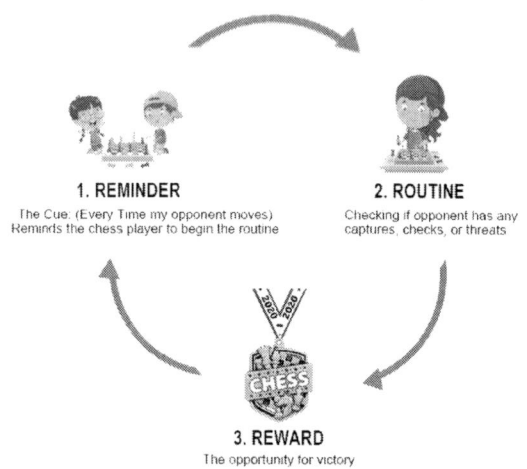

1. REMINDER
The Cue: (Every Time my opponent moves)
Reminds the chess player to begin the routine

2. ROUTINE
Checking if opponent has any captures, checks, or threats

3. REWARD
The opportunity for victory

3. Your reward is never being surprised by your opponent's moves.

4. The behavior you want to replace is losing and being upset for not seeing impending danger.

5. Don't beat yourself up if you miss a move; do it the following move. The point is the process.

Character

Good habits are not enough by themselves. To borrow a line from my favorite TV show, *Game of Thrones*, winter is coming!

When you think of winter, you may think of freezing cold temperatures, shivering, dressing in layers to protect yourself from the frigid temperatures, or snow up to your knees. Winter is a representation of adversity. Your habits will be tested by adversity.

Les Brown says, "Adversity introduces you to yourself."

Can you maintain habits under intense pressure? It depends on your character, which can be defined as a self-imposed commitment to a set of values, discipline, or standards without compromise for the sake of a higher purpose. Character protects your destiny from distractions, temptation, and adversity. It is the constant effort to integrate your words, actions, and deeds as one.

Character is the willingness to accept delayed gratification. As discussed in Chapter 1, your purpose is nothing to take lightly. It's what you dedicate your

life to. Your plans, goals, and objectives depend on it. When you become one, cues and triggers won't matter. It becomes a behavior you must—not should—do. Cues or no cues, you do it. Adversity or no adversity; you do it. Corona or no Corona; you do it. If you want to change your behaviors forever, you need character.

In Example 1 of the habit loop, you start your chores and homework when the alarm clock goes off. Having character means not needing the clock. What if the clock does not go off? What if there is no electricity or batteries (adversity)? Character is doing what you have to do anyway.

In the second example, what if you don't know your opponent's last move (the cue)? Character means always checking for captures, checks, or threats.

Having character may sound easy, but adversity will challenge your commitment to your plans, goals, objectives, and habits. No one is immune from adversity. It can't be stopped. Embrace it. Adversity is your vehicle to success. Your destiny is waiting for you.

Adversity is also an opportunity for greatness. Malcolm X passionately said, "There is no better than adversity. Every defeat, every heartbreak, every loss, contains its own seed, its own lesson on how to improve your performance next time."

Use adversity as the vehicle to your destination. Don't just go through it; grow through it. When we accept that there will be adversity, we grow and become who we are destined to be and arrive at our destination.

- ☑ Distractions are things that break your concentration and prevent you from winning and succeeding in your destiny, mission, and purpose.

- ☑ Internal distractions are your thoughts and emotions generated by your self-image and perceptions.

- ☑ External distractions are ones that originate outside of you.

- ☑ A situation creates thoughts and perceptions, thoughts produce feelings, feelings lead to your attitude, attitude becomes your character, and your character leads to your destination or destiny.

- ☑ When you focus—give full attention—on something, you minimize distractions.

- ☑ The habit loop is a neurological loop that governs any habit that consists of three elements: cue, routine, and reward.

- ☑ To change your behavior, you need to isolate and identify the cues and rewards you are looking for.

- ☑ Character is a self-imposed commitment to a set of values, disciplines, or standards without compromise for the sake of a higher purpose.

- ☑ Character solidifies habits by getting you through adversity and allowing you to stick to the plan.

- ☑ Use adversity as your source of inspiration and as a vehicle to success.

Chapter 5

Key Players: Acknowledge and Use All Resources

No one who achieves success does so without acknowledging the help of others.

~
Alfred North Whitehead

In the previous chapter, we discussed adversity and how to combat it by focusing, forming good habits, and maintaining character. This will help you overcome any adversity that could challenge your habits. The next part of your maturation is to see that you're not alone either. You should not face your challenges alone. Face them with everything you have. Do this by identifying and using every relevant form of support or assistance that is directly related

to the issue at hand. Make sure these sources can be verified and are accurate, and don't just use them individually but together.

Your resources should support and complement each other, as well as your plan, goals, and objectives. That is part of the holistic approach we have previously discussed. "No man is an island," and "It takes a village to raise a child," are both common sayings that illustrate this point.

Resource use refers to efficiently and effectively deploying and maintaining your resources. As we discussed in Chapter 3, effective means producing the desired result, while efficient means capable of producing desired results without wasting material, time, or energy. Being effective and efficient ensures that specific resources aren't being over or under-used. This will minimize the probability of abusing them. The worst thing you can do is misuse a resource because if you do, it won't be a resource for long.

To properly employ your resources, you must identify and assess them; deploy and position them most effectively and efficiently; appreciate, nurture,

and protect them; and be prepared to make tradeoffs and sacrifices.

Identify and Assess Your Personal Resources

Everything around you is an extension of you and is therefore a potential resource. Resources can generally be categorized into six classes: people, technology, material, boundaries, finances, and time. Let's get into each of them.

People

We, ourselves, are our first resource, along with our family, friends, adversaries, house of worship, community, colleagues, and mentors. We don't only benefit from others' physicality but also from their knowledge, experiences, wisdom, instincts, intuition, and insight as well.

B. J. Neblett said, "We are the sum total of our experiences."

And I'll add, we get access to them based on our network and relationships. Let's look at some of the concepts I just mentioned before.

To start with, knowledge. This refers to processed or comprehended information, it's more

than just mere exposure. Simply put, it's the things you think about. When you think about something, you compartmentalize it. You organize things in your mind so that they are easier to manage and retrieve when necessary.

Experience is a type of knowledge. It's the accumulation of knowledge or skill that results from direct participation in events or activities. It comes with time, exposure, and practice, and is based on its previous applications.

On the other hand, wisdom is the ability to know when, how, and where to use or not use the acquired knowledge. It's the process by which we judge between right and wrong, good and bad. Knowledge means understanding that a gun is a tool to protect yourself, while wisdom means knowing not to bring it to school.

Another resource you can use is instinct. Instinct comes from the Latin word for impulse, *instinctus*. Instinct is a hard-wired response: survival, reproduction, social, fight or flight, protecting our young. All animals, including humans, have instincts.

It's what makes babies cry to express pain, distress, and hunger.

Intuition is the ability to understand something immediately, without the need for conscious reasoning—your gut feeling. *Psychology Today* explains: "It's a form of knowledge that appears in consciousness without overt deliberation. It's not magic; just the unconscious mind rapidly sifting through past experience and cumulative knowledge."

Many people call intuition 'your sixth sense' because your intuition keeps you safe. It's your internal compass. It points you in the right direction. The sense that something is off about a particular thing or person, that's intuition. It's the way of knowing a thing beforehand and without needing to consciously analyze it because you do it at an unconscious level.

Insight, on the contrary, is the capacity to gain an accurate and deep intuitive understanding of a person or thing. *My dad is just getting off work and is probably tired and cranky. I'll ask him for the car when he has had some rest.* It's more person- and situation-specific.

Technology

Technology is science or knowledge put into practical use to solve problems or invent useful tools. It can be anything from the development of the wheel to computers and artificial intelligence. Modern examples are Twitter, computer applications, robotics, a coronavirus vaccine, a pneumatic drill, and electric cars. Any of these things can be used as resources to reach your goals.

Material

Material resources include all things that can be physically touched; nonmaterial resources like our feelings cannot be physically touched. Material resources can be as simple as paper, pens, textbooks, coats, gloves, and drinking cups.

Boundaries

Boundaries refer to things in your control area, dominion, purview, or scope—your space. It's a real or imagined line that marks the limit of something or the limit of a subject, principle, or relationship.

Control what you can control. You can't control other people, but you can control yourself and your

area. You control more by increasing your area or space. It is also important not to encroach on another's space or boundaries.

Financial Resources

These include money, bank deposits, and investments like stocks and bonds. Financial resources can't buy happiness, but they can buy security and safety for you and your loved ones. Human beings need financial resources to pay for all the things that make your life possible such as shelter, food, healthcare, and a good education.

Time

I've talked about time in this book multiple times, and this is because time is our greatest resource. It is universal. We all need and use it, and there is a limited supply of it. It's also a great equalizer: we can get more money, more knowledge, more skills, and more friends, more of almost anything, but we only get twenty-four hours per day no matter our race, religion, sexual preference, or economic status. No matter how high the demand,

the supply will not go up. And there is no substitute for it. We can substitute knowledge with money or vice versa, but not time.

Time is also our greatest adversary. It limits what we can achieve.

Develop and Deploy Your Resources

The second aspect of properly using your resources is positioning them for maximum effect. This speaks to when to use a resource and when not to, where to use them and where not to use them, and which resources work best together. This also relates to timing and compatibility of use. You know this through applied knowledge and wisdom as we discussed previously.

To develop and deploy resources optimally, you must assess them first. You must consider how they can be developed best; you must understand your desired roles for them, their inherent responsibilities and put them in a position to be successful.

Nurture and Protect Your Resources

The third component of tapping your resources is to appreciate, nurture, and protect them. One must appreciate them because they are scarce and not easy to come by.

You are your first resource. You must love and take care of yourself first. You can't nurture others if you are not healthy in mind and body. That's why the best ability is availability. This means taking care of yourself mentally, physically, and spiritually.

Most challenges that you'll confront in your life become opportunities the moment you realize that people can produce the solutions and answers you are searching for. It's these people who have the necessary knowledge, skills, experience, and resources you may need to help you turn a difficult situation into something that can help you move forward.

You must therefore continuously work on building and strengthening your relationships with key individuals on a daily basis in order to gain the necessary support. The law of attraction tells us that the best way to gain the support of others is to give them your support, especially during difficult times. Show them you are willing to go the extra mile, that

you are more than happy to provide them with value along with the solutions and answers they need to help improve their circumstances. The more you are willing to give to others, the more easily opportunities will come your way during difficult times.

Trade-Offs and Opportunity Costs

The fourth and final component of dealing with resources is to realize we must sometimes make trade-offs or sacrifices to realize our plans and goals. As discussed previously, resources are scarce, so we cannot get everything we want. We must choose some resources and give up others. We must be effective and efficient in our decision-making. We must compare the additional costs of alternatives with additional benefits. Most choices involve doing a little more or a little less of something; few choices are all or nothing decisions. This process creates trade-offs, and trade-offs result in opportunity cost.

A trade-off is when we sacrifice one resource to obtain another. We make trade-offs every day. It could be as simple as hitting the snooze button for

five more minutes of sleep and having to rush and possibly forget something when we are getting ready for school or work. It could be more complex, such as choosing between friends and jobs. When you make trade-offs, opportunity costs are created. Nothing is ever entirely free.

An opportunity cost is the result of the trade-off. It answers the question: *What must be given up as a result of choosing one over the other?* For example, if you are given $20 and choose to spend that money going to the movies, your opportunity cost will be everything else that you could have done with that $20, like buying candy, going to McDonald's, or saving the money altogether. You must always ask yourself: *Is it worth it?* If it is, take the opportunity; it is worth the cost. If it's not worth the cost, then it's not an opportunity; it's a distraction, and you shouldn't take it.

Identify and Assess Your Chess Resources

The board, and the pieces (material), the clock (time), computer engines, chess websites and computer apps (technology), people (represented by

chess books, your opponents, your experiences, coaches, videos), tournaments (money), and space.

How To Develop and Deploy Your Resources

This is covered more extensively in the chess rules book, but I will point out some basic tactics.

Develop your pieces. Move your pieces out from their starting squares into the game and get them ready for battle.

Don't make too many pawn moves.

Don't bring your queen out too early.

Don't move the same piece twice in the first eight to ten moves unless compelled to do so.

Castle early when possible and practical to do so.

Develop towards the center.

Clear your back rank and connect the rooks.

Chess Holism

By developing all your pieces and developing them toward the center, you can use them together. We previously discussed strategies and tactics. The more resources or pieces you have developed, the

more strategies and tactics you can employ. You will have more options available to you. You cannot checkmate the king with one piece. It always takes at least two, even if the other one is your opponent's piece getting in the way.

It's important to coordinate your pieces. The pieces should support and complement each other. They should work as one: this is the holistic approach. This involves improving your understanding of how pieces work together and what they can accomplish in conjunction. For example, possessing bishops of opposite colors allows you to control more squares and can be effective when both point toward your opponent's king's position. A queen and knight can be a great attacking pair. A helpful exercise is to set up an empty board and just move around different combinations of pieces to get a feel for how they can potentially interact.

Positionally, piece coordination can be improved by always asking whether your pieces are working well together. Ask yourself questions like:

If I move my rook to the c-file, will my advanced pawn lose an important defender?

If I move my knight to e4, will it block my bishop's influence on the diagonal?

A good habit is to always ask yourself questions while you play since it will help you determine better moves.

Appreciate, Nurture, and Protect Your Resources

You must appreciate, nurture, and protect your chess resources because – just as in life- they are scarce or not easy to come by. You only have eight pieces and eight pawns, sixty-four squares to work within, and however much time that has been mutually agreed on.

A reminder in reference to a numeric value, the queen is worth nine, rooks are worth five, knights and bishops are worth three, and pawns are worth one.

Not only does each piece except the king— have a numeric value, they each also have a situational value. There are circumstances in which a lower-valued piece may be more valuable than a higher numerically valued piece. For instance, a

knight is three points, but it could be more valuable than a five-point rook if it's protecting multiple important squares.

When you recognize something is scarce and therefore has significant value, you nurture it. This means you love, support, and protect it. If your opponent attacks one of your pieces, don't just ignore it; do something about it! You must make sure there is enough compensation in return.

Letting your opponent take all your pieces is one sure way to lose a game of chess. Of course, you can't protect all your pieces all the time, but it's generally a good idea not to leave too many pieces on unprotected squares. Too many unprotected pieces are recipes for disaster.

Tradeoffs and Opportunity Costs

A trade-off or sacrifice is when one player gives up a piece or position in exchange for one of lesser value and in return, they get some other advantage. While it is normally important to keep your pieces

safe and avoid having them captured, sacrifices can have great surprise value. If you blunder and lose a piece unintentionally and then happen to win the game anyway, that doesn't count as sacrifice! A sacrifice is intentional and occurs as part of a sequence of moves that includes other tactics. Sacrificing is a great way to decoy or deflect an enemy piece.

An opportunity cost is the result of the trade-off. It answers the question: *What must be given up as a result of choosing one over the other?* For example, if you are presented with a situation in which you must choose between allowing your opponent to take your knight or bishop, your opportunity cost will be what you could have done with the bishop or knight.

- ☑ To properly use your resources, you must: identify and assess each resource; deploy and position them most effectively and efficiently; appreciate, nurture, and protect them; and be prepared to make trade-offs and sacrifices.
- ☑ Resources can generally be categorized into six classes: people, technology, material, boundaries, finances, and time.
- ☑ People's resources are their knowledge, experiences, wisdom, instincts, intuition, and insight.
- ☑ Technology is the science or knowledge put into practical use to solve problems or invent useful tools.
- ☑ Material resources include all things that can be physically touched.
- ☑ Boundaries refer to things in your control area, dominion, purview, or scope.

- ☑ Financial resources include money, bank deposits, investments such as stocks and bonds.
- ☑ Time is our greatest resource. There is no substitute for it.

Chapter 6

Maintain Vigilance: Sustained Attention and Awareness

Expect the unexpected, believe the unbelievable, achieve the unachievable.

~
Unknown

The great motivational speaker Les Brown says, "You're either entering, in the middle of, or exiting a storm."

In life and chess, you will be under constant attack. Consequently, if you want to be successful at either or both, you must accept that there will always be adversity and be prepared to defend yourself against it at all times. Probably no other quote captures this feeling better than the Boy Scout motto: *Be prepared.* The question then becomes, what are we

preparing for? The answer is anything and everything. Perhaps the word that encapsulates the essence of being prepared for anything and everything best is *vigilance*.

The *Oxford Living Dictionary* defines vigilance as the action or state of keeping careful watch for possible danger or difficulties. The word derives from the Latin *vigilare*, which means *keep awake*. You must constantly stay awake to avoid danger and be ready to act at any time. Your game might depend on it. Your life may depend on it!

Being vigilant is like being a security guard watching over your most valuable possessions. The anticipation and preparedness they must have in case of an attack or danger is a vivid visual reference.

There are eight things you must do as good security guards in your life and chess to remain vigilant:

Reduce and/or avoid distractions.

Follow rules and procedures.

Recognize your strengths and weaknesses.

Observe your surroundings.

Trust your intuition.

Prepare for adversity.

Fight when necessary.

Learn from your experiences.

Reduce and/or Avoid Distractions

One of my good friends, retired police officer Lt. Col. Gerald Leyshock, frequently says, "Being distracted attracts criminals."

He is likening criminals to adversity because being a victim of crime creates mental and physical challenges. So being distracted attracts adversity. As you remember from Chapter 4, distractions are things that break your concentration and draw your attention from your chosen interest, plans, goals, and objectives onto something else. You may eliminate a distraction, but there will always be more distractions. Therefore, it's best to minimize their effect on you.

The way you do this is through focusing. This is concentrating all your attention and energy on a chosen goal. The keyword is *all*. This word is highlighted in the quote by life coach Art Williams:

"*All* you can do is *all* you can do. But *all* you can do is enough."

If you focus on your distractions, they will grow. If you give your full attention to your plan, goals, and objectives, they will also grow.

Therefore, you must use *all* your senses. For instance, think about how many times you normally

look at your cell phone, whether to reply to a text, check social media, or even look at directions while walking to a destination. In this case, your attention is divided, and you are therefore not using your relevant senses. You should be focusing only on getting to your destination. You should be looking, listening, smelling, feeling, and tasting if necessary. If you divide your attention, you may be unaware that a person could be following you. That person could be trying to rob or harm you, or both.

In chess, I can't tell you how many games I lost because I was watching TV, talking to someone, on my cell phone, or sleepy. These were distractions. I have also won many games because my opponent was distracted. The lesson I've learned that I'm passing on to you is that it's better to let your opponent be distracted than you.

Follow Rules and Procedures

Rules and procedures will guide you. You may not know what to do in every situation, but following rules and procedures is a great place to start. These are created as a guide to try and prevent negative things from happening or to increase the probability of a desired result occurring. Remember from Chapter 1, following rules and procedures is a form of humility and respect. It's an acknowledgment that others are smart and have valid perspectives. They can also prevent you from making the same mistakes that others have made before you.

The billionaire Warren Buffet said it best: "It's good to learn from your mistakes. It's better to learn from other people's mistakes."

For instance, if you obey the first rule of boxing and keep your hands up at all times, you will be in a position to defend punches seen and unseen. In chess, if you obey the principle of not bringing your queen out early, you can avoid her being trapped. If you castle early and develop your pieces, you can minimize tricky openings from your opponent.

This is applicable in real life as well. If you are in the house by 10:00 p.m., like your parents told you,

you won't have to worry about a drive-by shooting happening at 2:00 a.m.

Recognize Your Strengths and Weaknesses

Being aware of your strengths and weaknesses is imperative to being vigilant. Remember the SWOT analysis from Chapter 3? The main purpose of conducting a SWOT analysis is to increase success in a chosen activity by identifying your strengths, reducing or eliminating your weaknesses, using the opportunities, and minimizing or eliminating threats.

An ancient Greek popularized saying said, "Man, know thyself." If you know yourself, you know what you are good at and what you are not. You also know what things you need assistance with and additional relevant resources for. As my favorite childhood

cartoon G.I. Joe would say: *Knowing is half the battle. The other half is doing something about it.*

Once you know your strength and weaknesses, as Chapter 3 says, then you must implement strategies and tactics to reduce or eliminate your weaknesses and/or maximize the use of your strengths. For instance, in a game of chess if there is a particular opening, you don't perform well against, study it to get better. If you are really good with your bishop pairs, you strategically may not want to trade them for knights.

In life, if you know you don't perform well at the last minute, you should be proactive on your assignments and do things before they are due. If you know you love math and hate history, you might tutor others in math and get assistance from the instructor in history.

Observe Your Surroundings

Question everything. Questioning helps you to be more engaged with the world around you.

My friend, Lt. Col. Gerald Leyshock, has always advised me: "Be fully aware of your surroundings at all times."

You should ask questions like: *Why? Why not? Why now?* This is a great habit because it minimizes the possibility of being surprised by an event. You will more likely be prepared for adversity.

Sometimes the answers are easy and are common sense. Other times, they require deep thought and could even require assistance and additional resources. You won't know unless you ask.

In chess, every time your opponent moves, ask: *Why?* and *Am I in danger as a result of the move?* In life you might ask questions like: *Why is this person sweating, raising their voice, standing instead of sitting, wearing all red or blue*, etc.

If you use this method of thinking, you can get a handle on things before they snowball and get out of hand. It's much easier to handle easy problems rather than big ones. This habit also increases your self-

confidence because it forces you to find answers for yourself and not rely on others.

Trust Your Intuition

If the rules and procedures don't cover a circumstance and you don't have any relevant knowledge or experience regarding the matter, rely on your sixth sense, your intuition. Remember from Chapter 5 that intuition keeps you safe. It's your internal compass. It points you in the right direction, whether it's the sense that something is off about a particular thing or person, a fact that just doesn't add up, a situation seems perilous when it shouldn't, or easily finding patterns in things without conscious effort.

For instance, your intuition may be that it is going to rain today, and you should wear a raincoat,

even though the weatherman says otherwise. When it rains and you have on your coat, you'll look like a genius. Sometimes when I'm playing chess, my gut instinct may tell me not to take a piece or not move to a certain square. More often than not, my intuition is right, and my opponent has a nice trap for me.

You must also distinguish between fear of success or fear of failure and intuition. Intuition is unemotional and feels right. Fear of danger is good, natural, and instinctive. Fear of a loaded gun or fear of a tornado makes sense. On the other hand, fear of success or fear of failure hold you back and are mental blocks to success. This type of emotion is not intuition; it's a self-defeating behavior.

Prepare for Adversity

There is a Latin adage that says: *Si vis pacem, para bellum*, which translates to: *If you want peace, prepare for war*. War refers to adversity. When I was in the Army, we spent 99 percent of our time preparing for war. I thought it was the biggest waste of time.

My supervisor, Sergeant Thorpe, used to frequently say: *One day you'll be glad you did.*

Boy was he right. I found out that when the bullets start to fly, you don't have time to think. Your body will take over. You will rely on physical and mental muscle memory. All that training saved me and my fellow soldiers' lives.

This has also served me well in chess. When that clock is ticking, and my opponent is sweating bullets, I'm calm because I've been here before. I know what to do and what not to do.

Fight When Necessary

Sometimes confrontation is unavoidable. As my chess students say: *It is what it is.* If all else fails, be ready to fight but only when and as much as necessary. This is when all the training, rule-following, observing, focusing, and using all your senses pays off. You can be guilt-free and know it was a last resort. That being said, don't overdo it. Even if you can dominate your opponent, all life is precious and cannot be replaced.

One of the priests from the *Kung Fu* TV show said it best: "Check rather than hurt; hurt rather than maim; maim rather than kill."

Even in chess I try not to kill my opponent's spirit. Ultimately, it's all about sportsmanship and having fun.

Learn from the Experience

Always learn from every experience and encounter. As I continue to reiterate, time is our most valuable resource. We don't have it to waste.

As the evangelist Joel Osteen says, "Don't just go through it. Grow through it."

Look for feedback no matter how painful it may be to hear it. Grow through your experiences. Always strive to be better than you were yesterday. You need to realize that our failures fuel success. If you learn something, you can gain wisdom from it when used at the right time, place, or manner. It was not a waste of time, nor was it a waste of effort. Then you will be vigilant.

- ☑ Vigilance is always staying prepared to defend yourself against adversity.
- ☑ Be a good security guard in your life and chess.
- ☑ To continuously be vigilant: reduce and/or avoid distractions, follow the rules and procedures, recognize your strengths and weaknesses, observe your surroundings, trust your intuition, prepare for adversity, fight when necessary, and learn from your experiences.

Chapter 7

Actionize Opportunities

Opportunity is everywhere. The key is to develop the vision to see it.

~

Robin Sharma

The term actionize means to act upon or take action on. Actionizing opportunities is an active pursuit, not a passive one. You have to make it happen. In life and chess, when you follow the rules and principles, harmonize, create a plan, set goals and objectives, stick to your plan, use your resources effectively and efficiently, and maintain vigilance, opportunities for success will present themselves in abundance.

Many of these opportunities will be glaring and obvious, while others may be unrecognizable, unexpected, and hidden. They may be elusive and hard to recognize because they may come in various shapes and forms. They also may be dormant, hidden, and almost invisible, awaiting someone to create them.

The former prime minister of England, Benjamin Disraeli, eloquently stated: "The secret of success is to be ready when your opportunity comes."

In this chapter, we will discuss how to recognize, select, maximize, and create opportunities.

What Are Opportunities?

In Chapter 3 we discussed that an opportunity is anything that provides you with a chance to achieve your plan, goals, and objectives. Opportunity is also when timing meets your preparation. Therefore, to fully comprehend an opportunity, you must understand the importance of timing and preparation.

Timing is different from time. As stated, many times throughout this book, time is our most important resource. Time measures the duration of an event, like a chess match, or an action such as our life. We all need to use it properly since it's in limited supply.

On the other hand, timing maximizes the effect of that duration. When you have perfect or ideal timing, you get the most out of an event, action, or situation. When opportunities appear, you must recognize them and act upon them appropriately in a timely manner.

Preparation means to get ready for an occasion. The occasion is unseen opportunities. To be

prepared you must be optimally and appropriately developed. If you are not developed, you cannot take advantage of opportunities. This would be premature and opening yourself to being overwhelmed by adversity. As stated throughout this book, you must follow the rules and principles, harmonize, create a plan, set goals and objectives, stick to your plan, use your resources effectively and efficiently, and maintain vigilance.

What Do Opportunities Look Like?

Former NBA great Bill Walton said, "There are no guarantees in life. The simple twists of fate and the breaks of the game are the two maxims that define so much of the success and failure in life."

Sometimes, that's all you get: a chance or a possibility. You may just get a crack in the door. You must open the door yourself. As it relates to chess, it probably won't be a person blundering their queen. It will be more like a pawn, but it will be up to you to seize the opportunity and turn it into something.

In chess the two terms most closely related to timing are initiative and tempo. Tempo is an

opportunity to make a move you want to make and not be forced to make moves your opponent wants you to make. You are in control.

Initiative is making moves to make your opponent play reactively. Whoever has initiative is in control. If you are forced to respond to your opponent's moves before you can make the move you want, he has the initiative and tempo.

Recognizing opportunities is not always as easy as it may sound. Opportunities may be unrecognizable, unexpected, and hidden. They may be elusive and hard to recognize because they can take on various shapes and forms. The one consistent characteristic in all opportunities is that they always start with a choice. Take it or pass it up. Act on it or ignore it. It's a choice.

Our days are driven by decisions we often don't think twice about: Do you do your homework or not? Should you take this bus or wait for the next? *Should I trade a knight for a bishop? Should I castle to the king kingside or queenside? Which opening or defense should I use?* Each choice lends itself to numerous possibilities.

The question you must ask yourself when you are presented with a choice is: *Will this advance my mission, purpose, goals, and objectives?* If the answer is yes, then the next question should be: *Does it advance my mission, purpose, goals, and objectives effectively and efficiently?*

The answer must be yes to both effective and efficient. It's counterproductive if the choice is one and not the other. For example, I can drive to work while texting. This is quite efficient but not effective because my split focus could cause me to be in a fatal accident. Another example is if I wake up two hours early to get ready for school. I'm getting up early so I don't forget anything. I am never late. This is effective but not efficient. I could get my clothes ready for the week on Sunday. I could set alarms on my phone reminding me things not to miss.

Even if the choice is effective and efficient, it still may not be worth it. You must decide if it is worth it or not. You still must complete an opportunity cost assessment.

Opportunity Cost

We learned in Chapter 5 that nothing is free, not even opportunities. An opportunity cost is the result of an action taken. It answers the question: *What must be given up as a result of choosing one over the other?* You must always ask yourself if it is truly worth it. If you perceive that it is, take the opportunity.

Beware of pyrrhic victories. A pyrrhic victory is a victory that inflicts such a devastating toll on the victor that it is equal to defeat. Winning a pyrrhic victory takes a heavy toll that negates any true sense of achievement or damages long-term progress. If it's not worth the cost, then it's not an opportunity; it's a distraction and it must be avoided. Don't do it. Reconsider!

Fool's Gold

Things may not always be what they seem. The opportunity may be fool's gold. This is a common nickname for pyrite, which received that nickname because it's worth virtually nothing but has an appearance that fools people into believing that it's

real gold. So symbolically speaking, fool's gold is anything that appears to be worth more than it actually is. Opportunity fool's gold is a distraction.

Many times distractions can look like opportunities. Remember we highlighted in Chapter 4 that distractions break your concentration and draw your attention from your chosen interest, plans, goals, and objectives onto something else.

Distraction at its core is simply confusion about what matters. You must say no to distractions, no matter how enticing they may seem. If you do not, opportunities will flee from you, and misfortune, calamity, and regret will find you. You must be selective. You must say no to possibilities that are not in line with your purpose, plans, goals, and objectives.

BEWARE OF DISTRACTIONS DISGUISED AS OPPORTUNITIES

In chess a distraction is a decoy. Often a player might use a decoy to force the opponent to think about something else, while the player is actually focused on a different target entirely.

Deflection is a distraction tactic that keeps an opponent's piece from doing its job, such as defending an important square, pinning a piece, or blocking an open file or diagonal. Many decoy/deflection tactics involve a sacrifice or forcing a move of some kind, thus forcing the opponent to cooperate with the decoy/deflection tactic.

Positive Distractions

Not all distractions are bad. They can be rewards. You shouldn't wait until you get to the end of your journey to celebrate your successes and achievements. Celebrate all along the way.

There's a proverb that says: *Man does not live by bread alone.* That means human beings need more than the simple necessities to keep them alive biologically. They need things that feed them mentally, spiritually, aesthetically, and give their lives meaning. Even though you may need other things, don't go overboard.

Oscar Wilde captured it best when he said, "Everything in moderation, including moderation."

This means that you must avoid extremes. So, we can indulge in distractions, but don't overdo it. Don't

let them sabotage your mission, vision, plan, goals, and objectives.

Rewards can serve as simple, small, welcomed breaks. They need to be proportionate to your success. It also shouldn't take you out of your productive zone, the time and environment you get the most accomplished. You should have fun but not too much fun. You want to reward yourself for a reasonable time frame and amount.

Positive distractions can divert your attention from more harmful distractions. For example, playing a video game responsibly could keep you from hanging out with negative "friends." Lifting weights could divert your energy and time from illegal drug use. Writing and reading books can divert your attention from cheating on your companion.

Distractions can also be great motivators. They may be a distraction today but an opportunity tomorrow. As previously stated in this chapter, timing is extremely important. So, if you see something you want and you recognize that the time is not right for it, then you can plan and strategize for the right time.

For example, you might want a new car but have obligations that prevent you from getting it right now. Instead of indulging in the distraction of trying to impress others with your new car which would get you behind on your bills, you can work overtime to earn additional money to get the car.

This way, the car motivated your drive to work for long hours. Had you gotten it before its time, it would have been a distraction and could have caused you financial stress and hardship, which could have lead to physical, mental, and relationship concerns.

During a chess match, you may see a piece that is unprotected or minimally protected, and you want it. You can't go after it right now because you have not developed your pieces. So, you watch the piece, and if it is available later, you act on the opportunity.

Healthy Mental State

One of the primary reasons we don't always see opportunities when they are clear as day is because of our limited thinking. Our thinking is often limited because we are mentally frustrated or blocked. A mental block is the inability to remember or think of something you normally could; often caused by emotional tension or trauma, which is any negative life event that occurs when you feel helpless or hopeless.

If we are mentally blocked, it becomes difficult to think clearly and make appropriate decisions. Oftentimes our creativity and ingenuity are also blocked because we too frequently deal with adversity and trauma.

Psychologist Abraham Maslow illustrates this point in his hierarchy of needs theory.

In Maslow's hierarchy of needs, the highest level of psychological development usually occurs after basic needs have been met. He calls this self-actualization. It's hard to think about school if you are hungry and don't have a safe place to stay. It's hard to think about retirement when you don't have a job. It's hard to think about checkmating your

opponent when your pieces are not developed or your king is under attack. These needs are distractors that are too loud to ignore and must be satisfied if constant and fulfilling success is going to be achieved.

If we can satisfy the lower-level needs, then it will be easier to satisfy the higher level of needs. Altogether, there are five levels. These needs can also be transferred analogously to chess in the chess hierarchy of needs, as you can see below.

Abraham Maslow's "Hierarchy of Needs"

Self-Actualization
realizing personal potential

Esteem needs
prestige and feeling of accomplishment

Belonging and love needs
intimate relationships, friends

Safety needs
security, safety

Physiological needs
water, warmth, rest

"Chess Hierarchy Of Needs"

Chess-Actualization
realizing personal potential

Esteem needs
reward yourself productively, reasonably
propotionaly & constantly for achievements

Relationships
use all your resources effectively and efficiently

Safety needs
get your king to safety and protect your pieces at all times
and/or get adequate compensation for them

Basic needs
develop your pieces & toward the center of the board

Remember in Chapter 1 we emphasized looking at our beliefs and identifying any adverse beliefs that could potentially prevent us from taking advantage of opportunities. Believing in yourself affects everything you do—your professional life, your personal life, your relationship with yourself, and your choices.

It all starts with your mindset, with the conversations you have with yourself, and the messages you choose to believe. Remember, beliefs lead to thoughts, thoughts lead to feelings, feelings lead to actions, and actions lead to results. Your

reality is the reflection of your strongest belief. It's all up to you!

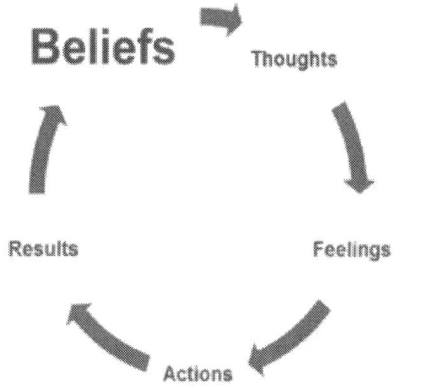

Lastly, you must be in a constant state of readiness. You must constantly be on the lookout for anything that could possibly help you achieve your goals and objectives far more quickly, effectively, or efficiently.

In chess, you should always be ready for a blunder or a passed pawn. It also means that you must be open to new perspectives and ideas, things out of the ordinary that could potentially provide you with unique understandings that will help move your goals forward or overcome the problems you are

facing. In chess, you shouldn't be scared to think outside the box. You should think about all combinations and exchanges as they could lead to unexpected positive positions.

Actionize Opportunities

Now that you know what opportunities are—and are not—and you are in the proper mental state, it's time to actionize your opportunities. When actionizing you are generally going to have some things in your way. You may have to remove some physical obstacles, the structural barriers in your environment that prevent or block mobility, access, and progress.

For example, if you can't see, you get glasses or contacts. If you can't hear, you get a hearing aid. If you can't go to an interview because you can't get a car, then you get an Uber or get on the bus. In chess, if a piece is preventing you from checkmating your opponent, you sacrifice another piece, even if it's the queen. You must use everything at your disposal.

Just as stated in Chapter 5, you must use all your relevant resources to achieve success. Remember,

resources are sources of support or assistance that are directly related to the issue at hand, can be verified, and are accurate. We should use, develop, and enhance our knowledge, experiences, wisdom, instincts, intuition, and insight.

B. J. Neblett says, "We are the sum total of our experiences."

In any given situation, these resources will guide us on what to do or not do.

We must use, develop, and enhance our creativity and imagination. Creativity is the use of imagination

or original ideas to create something. Creative thinkers tend to find better opportunities in life. Even though some may say this is just good luck, the truth is that opportunities come to creative people because they look for them until they find them. Every advancement started with a new idea, and new ideas are inspired by imagination and creativity. If you find creative answers to these questions, more opportunities will keep coming along.

We will also need to use, develop, and enhance our strategies and tactics. Your strategy is your how. How will you achieve your goal in a specific position or situation? Tactics primarily deal with observation and calculation. Tactics are patterns, combinations, or tricks developed to drive and support the strategy and to get you closer to the objective.

In a chess match you should try to deflect and legally distract your opponent (not with noises and physical movements). Distract your opponent's piece from doing its job, such as defending an important square, pinning a piece, or blocking an open file or diagonal. Sacrifice a piece or pieces to gain an advantage or higher-valued piece. Implement a move

of some kind that forces your opponent to move to an undesired position for your tactical gain.

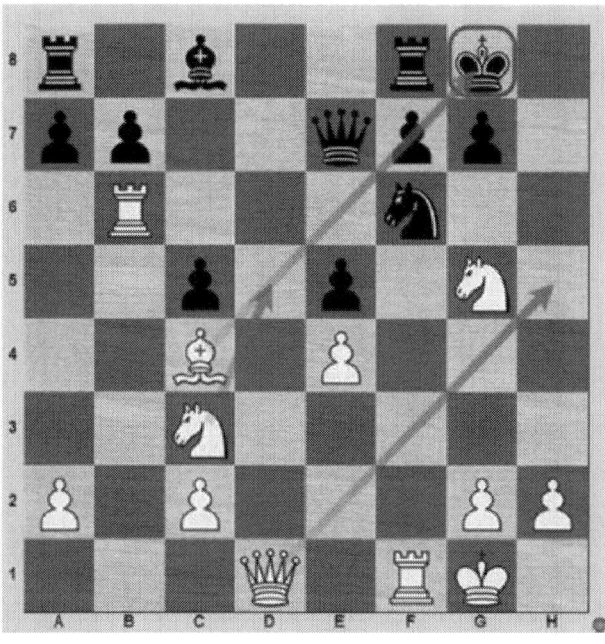

We may even need to change our environment. This environment at a minimum might not support change, or even worse, it could discourage change. Your environment, which includes your friends, colleagues, location, habits, and lifestyle, impacts you far more than you realize. But when you make incremental improvements to your environment, it becomes much easier to do what's right. When you

have better options within reach, it becomes the default choice.

The new environment doesn't have to be positive. It can be neutral or adverse. An adverse environment could also assist you, like juvenile detention. In detention—away from a negative environment—you have a lot of time for introspection and thinking. To do something out of the ordinary may require a lot of willpower, which you may not have. Restrictions may enhance your thinking and problem-solving abilities. It might also force you to reexamine your daily routines and what you should be doing and not doing.

Learn from Your Opportunities

 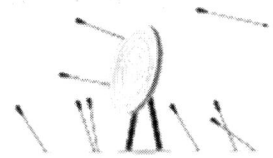

Finally, as Joel Osteen says, "Don't just go through it, grow through it."

Whether you successfully take advantage of an opportunity or not, it's paramount that you take time to analyze what you did, what went wrong, and how you could take better advantage of similar opportunities in the future. That is the whole point of lifelong learning and could very well be the key to success in any field of human endeavor.

Qualities to Help You Take Advantage of Opportunities

Curiosity. An opportunity requires a curious mind that is always asking deeper and more insightful questions.

Generosity. Due to the law of attraction, seizing an opportunity may require that you give opportunities to others—of course not during a chess match.

Perseverance. Having determination; persisting and persevering despite the seemingly insurmountable obstacles that stand in their way will help you seize opportunities.

Confidence. Opportunity benefits from a confident demeanor from someone who never doubts their skills, strength, resources, and abilities.

Optimism. If you have an optimistic attitude that doesn't waver off course if things don't go as expected, you'll be more likely to successfully seize your opportunities.

Playfulness. Opportunity also requires a lighthearted approach and a willingness to be a little creative; to think outside the box, and to break conventional rules.

Responsibility. Someone who's fully committed and responsible for their decisions, behavior, and actions is someone who doesn't make excuses or

throws blame on others. Opportunities require taking responsibility.

Foresight. Opportunity needs someone with foresight who can see beyond this fleeting moment into the future. That someone understands that what might look like a problem now might actually be a once-in-a-lifetime opportunity.

Patience. Change usually doesn't happen overnight. It takes time. You must be patient. Patience shifts your attention away from stress, anxiety, and frustration, showing confidence in our vision, plan, goals, and objectives.

- ☑ Actionizing opportunities means to act on and take advantage of opportunities when they present themselves.
- ☑ An opportunity is anything that provides you with a chance to achieve your plan, goals, and objectives. Opportunity is also when timing meets your preparation.
- ☑ The one consistent characteristic in all opportunities is that they always start with a choice.
- ☑ You must evaluate the opportunity cost. Ask yourself if it is worth it.
- ☑ Beware of distractions disguised as opportunities (fool's gold). They'll break your concentration and draw your attention from your chosen interest, plans, goals, and objectives.

- ☑ Positive distractions are good if used in moderation, reasonably, and timely.
- ☑ You must always be in a healthy mental state to see the opportunities.
- ☑ To remove physical barriers to your opportunities you must be prepared to use relevant resources, change environments, and develop, and enhance your strategies, tactics, creativity, and imagination.
- ☑ You must learn from opportunities. Don't just go through it, grow through it.

Chapter 8

Tune-Up: Sharpen Your Axe

Give me six hours to chop down a tree, and I will spend the first four sharpening the ax.

~
Abraham Lincoln

Do you feel sluggish mentally and/or physically? Do you feel like you are just going through the motions? Do you feel like you are not advancing in life and/or chess at the pace you desire? Do you feel like you are not working with purpose? Are you unable to resolve conflicts and have difficulty controlling your anger?

If you said yes to any or all of these questions, you might just need a personal tune-up—to sharpen your ax. The areas in our lives that need sharpening

and tuning up the most are our mind, body, social selves, and spirit.

We can't complete our mission if we're not around to complete it. We can't complete our mission if we're not effective and efficient. We have discussed in detail that time is our enemy, and we therefore have to be effective and efficient with our time. And how can you do this if you are not in your best mental, physical, spiritual, and social condition? You can't be effective and efficient in life, chess, or any endeavor if any of those areas are unbalanced.

As we discussed in Chapter 7, according to Maslow's hierarchy of needs, the highest level of psychological development usually occurs only after previous needs have been met. Likewise, you can

only advance in chess if the lower-level needs are met in the chess hierarchy of needs. Some people never meet all their needs and reach self-actualization. Those who are fortunate enough to reach it only do so for a period of time and need an adjustment, sharpening, or tuning-up periodically.

"Chess Hierarchy Of Needs"

Chess-Actualization
realizing personal potential

Esteem needs
reward yourself productively, reasonably propotionaly & constantly for achievements

Relationships
use all your resources effectively and efficiently

Safety needs
get your king to safety and protect your pieces at all times and/or get adequate compensation for them

Basic needs
develop your pieces & toward the center of the board

Abraham Maslow's "Hierarchy of Needs"

- **Self-Actualization** — realizing personal potential
- **Esteem needs** — prestige and feeling of accomplishment
- **Belonging and love needs** — intimate relationships, friends
- **Safety needs** — security, safety
- **Physiological needs** — water, warmth, rest

In this chapter we will discuss what a tune-up is, signs that show you need a tune-up, and how and when you should get a tune-up in any of the four areas previously mentioned.

The Ax Parable

According to Ecclesiastes 10:10 in the Bible, "If the ax is dull and its edge unsharpened, more strength is needed, but skill will bring success."

Once upon a time, a very strong woodcutter asked for a job in a timber mill. The woodcutter was determined to do his best. His boss gave him an ax and showed him the area where he would work. The first day, the woodcutter cut eighteen trees.

"Congratulations," the boss said.

Motivated by the boss's words, the woodcutter tried even harder the next day, but he could only cut fifteen trees. The third day he tried even harder, but he could only cut ten trees. Day after day, he finished with fewer trees.

I must be losing my strength, the woodcutter thought.

He went to the boss and apologized, saying that he could not understand what was going on.

"When was the last time you sharpened your ax?" the boss asked.

"Sharpen? I've had no time to sharpen my ax. I have been so busy trying to cut trees."

The moral of this story is that working hard by itself is not the recipe for success. You must be effective and efficient as well. You don't want to waste any effort or energy. Inefficient tools waste your energy. It's better to spend the majority of your time finding and cultivating the best tools for any task.

In the most literal sense, this story is about keeping your equipment in good working order and

taking time to maintain your equipment. In a more theoretical sense, it's about continuous self-improvement. It's about taking care of yourself—your whole you: mind, body, emotions, and soul. This is known as the holistic approach.

In this story the woodcutter was effective and efficient on the first day. Each day he became less effective and efficient. He did not use all his relevant resources. Every profession has standards, procedures, and trends. It is the woodcutter's job to keep up with these standards and trends in his profession. Also, the boss was a resource. He could have asked the boss for help sooner. He could have also been more of an effective listener. The boss gave him advice, he heard him, but he did not actively listen. Active listening means processing, and concentrating on what you hear in order to understand the message. You should also ask questions when you don't understand. That way you get clarity. The woodcutter needed a tune-up!

Personal Tune-Up

Sometimes we forget where we're going and why we're going there. We need reminders. We need a tune-up. A personal tune-up—sharpening our saw—is increasing our personal growth with self-care and self-maintenance. Regardless of our station in life, we all need regular personal tune-ups. No one is perfect, and we all have room for improvement, aka a personal tune-up.

Personal growth helps you improve your weaknesses. It gives you the opportunity to take an honest look at the areas of your life that need improvement. Through this process, you get to know who you really are, what your true values are, and where you would like to go in life. It also helps you develop your strengths. By taking time to focus on nurturing and using your strengths more, you go

from being good at chess and/or life to being excellent at it.

German writer and poet, Johann Wolfgang von Goethe, summed it up best when he said, "We must always change, renew, rejuvenate ourselves; otherwise, we harden."

He is saying we must be flexible, open-minded, and willing to learn. We won't gain new understanding and open the doors to new opportunities that may have been closed if we remain rigid and hard. The more we learn, the more we grow, and the more we grow, the more adaptable we become.

How Do You Know When You Need a Tune-Up?

Being the healthiest version of yourself means taking care of your mind, body, emotions, and spirit. There will always be signs when a tune-up is needed. For example, in a car the dashboard lights may come on, you may hear and feel unusual noises or vibrations, or your car won't accelerate like it used

to. We are no different. Our bodies and environment will give us signs that we need a tune-up

If you need a mental tune-up, you may have headaches, depression, lack of focus, or anxiety. If your body needs a tune-up, you may have a temperature over 102, a consistent cough, aches and pains, or a lack of stamina.

If you need an emotional tune-up, you might be blaming others for your problems, have difficulty resolving conflicts, lack meaningful connections with others, have difficulty controlling your anger and frustration, or lack empathy and compassion for others.

If you need a spiritual tune-up, you may not appreciate life or others, have no purpose or direction, don't help others, don't meditate, or don't spend time with yourself.

How Do You Get a Tune-Up in Each of the Four Areas?

Your mind, body, social self, and spirit all work together. While each is separate, they are all connected. There is an interdependence between

each area. Therefore, when thinking of renewing or tuning-up any of these areas, it's best to think in a holistic manner. Find activities and solutions that can sharpen or improve more than one area simultaneously. Thinking holistically recognizes the ripple effect. One action causes another, which then causes a third and so on.

The Mind

"Eventually, your cognitive skills will wane, and thinking and memory will be more challenging, so you need to build up your reserve," says Dr. John N. Morris, director of social and health policy research at the Harvard-affiliated Institute for Aging Research.

The goal of tuning-up your mind is to continue expanding your mind to maximize use of it today and to prepare for this eventual decline tomorrow. Keeping the brain active is an important aspect of mental health.

The more you use your brain, the better your mental operations become. Brain activities are a great way to maintain your overall mental health. Challenging mental activities stimulate the formation

of new nerve cell connections and may encourage new cell generation. Two great brain exercises are keeping a journal of your thoughts, experiences, and insights, and reading.

Start a gratitude journal.

It's a funny thing about life; once you begin to take note of the things you are grateful for, you begin to lose sight of the things that you lack. ~ Germany Kent.

Writing down your everyday experiences helps in identifying various mistakes that have been made or decisions that have proven to be unfruitful. More importantly, it is also a great motivator, as you can look at your successes as well. In chess, this way of documenting is called notation. Whether in life or chess, this exercise will allow you to clarify the future

course of action that will enable you to achieve your goals.

Read, Read, Read ...

According to English poet and playwright Joseph Addison, "Reading is to the mind what exercise is to the body."

This mental exercise improves intelligence, vocabulary, memory, and empathy and wards off mental decline. Reading introduces you to new words, which advances your vocabulary. A larger range of vocabulary is linked to higher test scores. Reading forces us to pay attention, remember small details, and follow along for hours at a time. Reading helps you relate with the characters and understand

their struggles, which in turn helps increase empathy. Reading helps ward off mental decline and dementia symptoms. "Studies show that people who read regularly have a 32% lower chance of mental decline as compared to those who don't read" (Gordon).

You should read whatever and whenever you can. Technology makes reading very easy today. You can read on tablets, laptops, and even your phone. You can read fantasy or science fiction to escape reality. If you're trying to improve your chess game, chess tactics and grandmaster games are a great choice. You can read some non-fiction to educate and motivate yourself. Whatever you decide, just read!

The Body

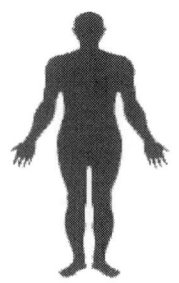

Our most important asset is our body and its health and wellness. We cannot achieve, plan, or reach our destiny, goals, and objectives if our body cannot support us. The goal of continuous physical improvement is to exercise our body in a way that will enhance our capacity to work, adapt, and enjoy life.

The benefits of physical fitness are many. It keeps your muscles and bones strong, controls your weight, disease-proofs your body, improves your mood and brain function, helps you sleep better, and boosts your energy and confidence.

It is important that you pick the right types of exercise for you. Most people benefit from a combination of them:

"**Endurance or aerobic** activities increase your breathing and heart rate. They keep your heart, lungs, and circulatory system healthy and improve your overall fitness. Examples include brisk walking, jogging, swimming, and biking" (Exercise and Physical Fitness).

Strength or resistance exercises make your muscles stronger. Some examples are lifting weights and using a resistance band.

Balance exercises can make it easier to walk on uneven surfaces and help prevent falls. To improve your balance, try tai chi or exercises like standing on one leg.

Flexibility exercises stretch your muscles and can help your body stay limber. Yoga and doing various stretches can make you more flexible.

Social

According to the English poet and scholar, John Donne, "No man is an island entire of itself; every man is a piece of the continent, a part of the main."

This means we are all connected, we are not meant to be isolated from others, and need to be part

of a community to be our best selves. If we are destined to be part of a community, then we must learn about ourselves and others. We must develop meaningful relationships.

The goal of tuning-up ourselves socially is to develop more meaningful relationships and/or enhance the ones we currently have. A meaningful relationship is based on mutual respect and supportiveness and is marked by a sense of commitment and fulfillment.

"Meaningful relationships play a vital role in overall well-being. Research has shown that individuals with supportive and rewarding relationships have better mental health, higher levels of subjective well-being, and lower rates of morbidity and mortality" (Lesnansky).

Ten Ways to Build Meaningful Relationships

1. Be happy with yourself. Holistic health coach, Michelle Maros, said it best: "Your relationships outside will flounder if you don't have unconditional love and compassion for yourself."

2. Listen to understand instead of to reply. Make eye contact, don't interrupt, repeat what they said, and respond to what they said.

3. Be positive and laugh often. People would rather be around someone who is positive and upbeat. Laughter is contagious.

4. Get rid of negative relationships. Letting go of unnecessary relationships opens up the opportunity to let new relationships into your life.

5. Find common interests. Common interests can bring you together, and differences in interests can separate you.

6. Learn to trust others. Trust is the foundation for any relationship. Without it, you won't feel secure, and security is a basic need.

7. Set clear expectations. It eliminates or reduces confusion and sets boundaries.

8. Don't be judgmental. No one wants to be judged. When you judge you tend to try to correct, convince, control, or change someone else.

9. Be patient. Patience shows you care, and caring builds trust.

10. Don't sweat the small stuff. It makes you a happier person. You live longer, and people want to be around you more.

Spirit

The spiritual element of wellness can be the most personal piece of the puzzle when trying to place all four areas of wellness together. Generally, people like to live a life with meaning and purpose. When these goals are met, it puts harmony in one's life and the people they surround themselves with. Christina Puchalski, director of the George Washington Institute for Spirituality and Health, contends, "Spirituality is the aspect of humanity that refers to the way individuals seek and express meaning and purpose and the way they experience their

connectedness to the moment, to self, to others, to nature, and to the significant or sacred."

The goal of a spirituality tune-up is to get us closer to our purpose, connections, nature, and what we hold sacred.

There are seven ways to improve your spiritual wellness. It's best to figure out what techniques work best for you. Since spiritual wellness involves one's values, beliefs, and purpose, it can be achieved in several ways, both physically and mentally.

Explore your spiritual core. By exploring your spiritual core, you are simply asking yourself questions about the person you are and your meaning. Ask yourself: *Who am I? What is my purpose? What do I value most?* These questions will lead you down a road where you will think more in-depth about yourself and allow you to notice things about yourself that will help you achieve fulfillment.

Look for deeper meanings. Looking for deeper meanings in your life and analyzing occurring patterns will help you see that you have control over

your destiny. Being aware of this can help you achieve a happy and healthy life.

Get it out. Expressing what is on your mind will help you maintain a focused mind. After a long day or a significant event, you may feel confused and not be able to make sense of your feelings. By writing down your thoughts, you may be able to think clearer and move forward.

Try yoga. Yoga is a physical technique that can help improve your spiritual wellness by reducing emotional and physical strains on your mind and body. Yoga is taught at all different levels and can help lower stress, boost the immune system, and lower blood pressure as well as reduce anxiety, depression, fatigue, and insomnia.

Travel. Taking time for yourself to travel to a comforting place or somewhere new can do wonders for your mind. When you are at a place where your mind can keep out distractions and help you reflect and rest, you will have a better connection with yourself. This allows you to weed out stressors and set your mind on the right path for overall wellness.

Some activities to take part in when on a trip can be exercising, speaking with a counselor or advisor, meditation, or taking a temporary vow of silence.

Think positively. Once you start viewing things in your life in a positive manner, you will find yourself thinking differently and refocusing your mind to a happy, healthy place. When you eliminate negativity and reframe how you think of certain things and situations, you'll notice yourself becoming more relaxed.

Take time to meditate. While managing your time and daily tasks can be hard, it is crucial to devote time to connect with yourself. Whether it is in the morning when you wake up, during your lunch break, or before you go to sleep, take five to ten minutes to meditate each day. Fitting meditation and relaxation into your lifestyle will free your mind and foster a stronger relationship with your spiritual wellness.

- ☑ A personal tune-up (sharpening your axe) is increasing your personal growth with self-care and self-maintenance.
- ☑ The areas in our lives that need sharpening and tuning-up the most are our mind, body, social selves, and spirit.
- ☑ Your body and/or environment will let you know when you need a tune-up.
- ☑ Think holistically. There is an interdependence and connection between each area.
- ☑ The more you use your brain, the better your mental operations become. Two great brain exercises are keeping a journal of your thoughts, experiences, and insights and reading.
- ☑ Physical fitness keeps your muscles and bones strong, controls your weight, keeps your body away from diseases, improves your mood,

improves brain function, helps you sleep better, and boosts your energy and confidence.
☑ A meaningful relationship is based upon mutual respect and supportiveness and is marked by a sense of commitment and fulfillment.
☑ The spiritual element of wellness is to live a life with meaning and purpose.

References

Gordon, Alycia. "7 Ways Reading Can Help Your Mental Health." *Awaken the greatness within*, https://www.awakenthegreatnesswithin.com/7-ways-reading-can-help-your-mental-health/. Accessed15 January, 2021.

"Exercise and Physical Fitness." *MedlinePlus*, https://medlineplus.gov/exerciseandphysicalfitness.html#:~:text=Endurance%2C%20or%20aerobic%2C%20activities%20increase,exercises%20make%20your%20muscles%20stronger. Accessed15 January, 2021.

Lesnansky Lori, "How to Make Your Relationships More Meaningful." *Cara Podcast*, 5 November 2020, https://www.buzzsprout.com/912259/6236833-how-to-make-your-relationships-more-meaningful

Chapter 9

Enlighten Others

The best way to find yourself is to lose yourself in the service of others.

~
Mahatma Gandhi

Every day we should strive to reach our full potential. This is not the amount of money, cars, or homes we acquire but the number of people we help along the way on our journey. We are created to serve and help others. True success is therefore measured by the number of lives we positively affect. We are who we help. This is especially true with our children, as they are our greatest asset and future.

Youth advocate, Josh Shipp, says it best: "Every kid is one caring ... [person] away from being a success story."

Oftentimes their genius is camouflaged as an annoyance. As leaders and mentors, we just have to redirect the annoyances and cultivate their talent. Every man, woman, or child can be a mentor and help others. There is only one quality necessary to be a mentor, and that is showing care. In this chapter I will share my experiences on how I poured myself into some kids I encountered. I gave them my most valuable resource, which is my time. I dared to care.

Never Say Never

One of the youth residents at the juvenile detention center I work at, TB, is thirteen. Despite his youth, he is one of the most difficult residents I have ever encountered. He was confined for more than six months. During that time, he assaulted at least nine staff members, threw a chair through a window, flooded his cell by trying to flush clothes and blankets down his toilet more times than I care to remember, and said more curse words on a daily

basis than I have hairs on my head. As staff, we were at our wit's end with him. Nothing worked. It looked like there was no hope for him to change.

One day, he said to me, "Teach me chess, fat ass."

I told him to ask someone skinny to teach him since he was disrespectful, stressing that I wouldn't teach him anything until he changed his behavior. He then apologized. A few days later, he asked me again, and I reluctantly agreed.

It was on a Wednesday, and I vividly remember it like it was yesterday. I taught him some chess theory, the basic rules, and how the pawns move.

On Saturday, when I returned to work, he said, "I read a chess book and know how to play chess now."

He also said that he had beaten some of the staff members. This sounded ridiculous and improbable. He assured me he was saying the truth. He even swore it on his gang. At that point, I started to believe him because the kids in the facility rarely lie in the name of their gang. I asked around, and everyone

said it was true. I still didn't believe him, so TB and I played a game. Then another one and another. I was pleasantly amazed by his advance in such a short period of time. He could not beat me, but he could play a competitive game. I had never seen anyone pick the game up that quickly.

Over the next few weeks, I taught him more and more. He was picking up everything like a sponge. What was even more amazing was that he had no more write-ups. Was he perfect? No, but his behavior had significantly improved. I would have never imagined he would have been my greatest student, not to mention that chess would play such an instrumental role in his maturation process. I dared to care.

Andrea Strong

One of my chess students, Andrea, texted me one night and said she was thinking of committing suicide. Having a degree in psychology and formerly worked as a suicide hotline counselor, I knew that the number one thing you must do is keep the person talking. So that was exactly what I did. I talked to her

for more than two hours until I was reasonably confident that she was okay.

The next morning, I alerted the principal and social worker of the situation. They talked with her and her family about the circumstances, and I'm happy to say that she is still with us. That was a difficult situation for me because she was my student, and I did not know if she was going to be upset with me for informing others about her situation. In the end, I had no choice because her life meant more to me than our relationship.

Kids can be so amazingly resilient. When I saw her later that day, she said she was okay and even came to chess practice. Over the next week she didn't miss a single practice. The following week we had a chess match. You could certainly tell that Andrea was ready for the match. She had taken to chess like fish to water and was one of my best players.

Close to the end of her chess match, I looked across the room and saw her in a dominating position. She had the opposing king trapped on the back rank with her king and queen. We had gone

over this exact position extensively during practice, and she did exceedingly well. I felt confident that she would win easily.

Before I could reach the board, the opposing player raised his hand and said, "I can't move."

I can still hear those words ringing in my ear. It was a draw. We tied a game we should have clearly won. We lost every other match that day.

This match's outcomes were devastating to the team. Many of the team members threatened to quit. In fact the next day, only one person showed up for practice. I spent the next twenty-four hours trying to put the team back together. I felt like Humpty Dumpty.

I implored them not to give up; we didn't come this far to give up. I used every motivational cliché I could think of:

The harder you work, the harder it is to surrender. The future is purchased by the present.

If we would put in the work, then we can be great. We just have to pay our dues and honor the struggle.

Our proverbial container can only hold 100 percent, and we can't afford to have negativity and doubt in our container.

The road to success is paved with failure. Failing is part of being successful. Often, we fail more times than we succeed.

We had to change our attitude. If we have a better attitude, then we are guaranteed better results.

It worked. The following day, everyone came back to practice. It was a great week of practice. And everyone showed up to each practice with enthusiasm. We went over the queen-king ending extensively, among other positions, and I felt confident we were prepared for the next tournament.

Finally, it was game day. There was a feeling of new hope in the air as we were back on the road to success. The team had been through a lot of adversity over the past week, especially Andrea, but it felt like we were a team. As we began to play, we lost the first and third boards but won the second and fourth. It came down to the final board. If we won the game,

we'd win the match. If we lost or tied the game, we'd lose the match.

Wouldn't you know it was Andrea, the same young lady who drew her game the previous week. During the game I walked over to her and found that she was in an even more dominating position than last week. She had a rook, knight, bishop, a queen, and about six pawns, while the opponent only had a lone king. I thought to myself that it would be a drawn game because there were minimal places for the king to move.

But there was something different about her that week. There was a sense of confidence that permeated the air. She wasn't rushing, and her every move was slow and deliberate. What was also surprising about her play was that she was only moving the queen and king even though she had an assortment of ancillary pieces.

It was as though she said to herself: *I will checkmate this king with my queen and king.*

She was committed. She wanted to prove something to herself. She pushed the opponent's

king to the edge of the board with her queen and king until there was nowhere left to run, and she said the majestic word.

"Checkmate!"

We won thirteen to twelve. This was easily one of my proudest coaching moments.

I dared to care.

Chess Is More Contagious Than the Coronavirus

The coronavirus has forever changed the world. It is so contagious that it has affected every area of our lives—our homes, education, recreation, mental health, religion, employment, food, and so on.

One of the places it has affected me personally is my workplace. I work in a juvenile detention center, and several of the youth have contracted the virus. Consequently, all movement in the facility has been minimized to reduce the spread of the virus. As a result, the youth are spending more time in their cells.

Studies have proven that mental health is negatively affected by extended periods of solitary

confinement. So we were tasked with finding creative ways to interact with the offenders without increasing physical contact. As an avid chess player and instructor, my first thought was my Swiss army knife—chess. I discussed the idea of playing with the offenders from their cells with my supervisors, and they loved and supported the idea.

The idea was the first hurdle, but how would I implement this? I had some barriers to overcome: the physical barrier of the cells and the minimal interest of the youth.

As a way of motivating myself, I authored a quote, "Be detoured, not deterred."

It means finding a way to do the things we desire to do, no matter how arduous the task may seem. There were seven offenders in my unit, and they primarily rap and write raps all day during their free time. I asked all the youth if any of them played chess. My experience is that most people will say yes, even if they only know how to move the pieces.

One of the youth said, "Yes, and I will beat you."

I quickly sprayed the chess pieces down with disinfectant, put on my gloves and mask, and sat down in front of the clear glass of the cell door of my unsuspecting opponent.

I explained to him what the letters and numbers meant on the chessboard and how he could use that to tell me where he wanted to move. So we began.

We were having so much fun that other youth started asking, "Can I play next?"

I started playing with three of the seven. Then I thought: *What if I give each of them a board? They could yell through the walls to play with each other.*

Over the next week, six of the seven started playing every day. Now when I walked into the unit, instead of profanities being yelled, I heard things like: *Knight to C3, queen take your queen, and checkmate.*

They woke up playing and went to sleep playing. I literally had to tell them that if they didn't go to bed, I would take their chess sets.

One of the kids told me, "I put him in a mean checkmate, something terrible [creatively and he did not see it coming]."

It didn't stop there. Other staff members also played with the youth and even got lessons from me. The transformation was just amazing. Chess is truly more contagious than the coronavirus.

I dared to care.

Twenty Is Greater Than COVID-19

I was a summer camp chess assistant instructor for a police and chess mentoring program from June to July in the summer of 2020. This program addresses the need for improved relationships between at-risk kids and police officers in the community.

Anyone who turns on the TV can see this was truly needed. Whether it's George Floyd, Brianna Taylor, Eric Garner, or Michael Brown, it's clearly a pervasive problem in America. The unique program pairs police officers with at-risk school children to teach chess and play together either in schools, at organized tournaments, or detention centers. The program also provides officers with the knowledge and tools to act as an ongoing resource to help further programs in schools.

During the summer program, the head instructor's mother passed away due to COVID-like symptoms. In order to keep the program going, I took over as the lead instructor. We have a next man up mentality. We support each other and are always ready to assist each other no matter the adversity. This was no different. We were not going to let COVID-19 beat us in 2020. Our motto became *Twenty is greater than nineteen.*

The month-long program had eighteen participants ranging from the age of ten to seventeen, who were paired with four police officers. Most of the participants were novice chess players—at best. I taught them the basics of chess using the associative learning method between chess and life. This method had been so successful for me as an instructor. I found that my students retained the information better and stayed engaged throughout the program.

To my surprise, during the summer two of the former residents of the juvenile detention facility where I work, L and C, were attending a mandated job-readiness program in the same building. I would

see them daily and motivate and joke with them during the breaks. Of course, they would always falsely claim they could beat me in chess. They would come by periodically to talk and play a game of chess during lunch.

We gave out certificates to students who finished the summer program. They had to stand in front of the group and answer a series of chess questions correctly to receive their certificate. L and C asked if they could take the test and get a certificate too.

Of course, I said yes. I love it whenever kids are excited about chess. Amazingly, they took the test and got a certificate as well, even though they did not attend the full program.

Nothing can stop a motivated child.

Something occurred to me: we had eighteen participants before L and C joined, but now we had twenty. It was uncanny and symbolic that we had exactly twenty participants. If this camp was successful, then twenty really could beat nineteen.

L and C also requested to participate at the end of the camp chess tournament. There were twenty

participants. Wouldn't you know it, L and C placed in the tournament, finishing second and fourth respectively.

You don't have to finish first to be a winner, you just have to give it all you have. You win with the experience and knowledge you gain.

Nelson Mandela said it best: "I never lose. Either I win or learn."

It was a great tournament and camp. Twenty was truly greater than nineteen.

I dared to care.

Final Thoughts

Just play. Have fun. Enjoy the game.

~

Michael Jordan

Enjoy your life and chess journey. While they can both be daunting, hard, and overwhelming at times, they can also be wonderful, amazing, and rewarding. Perhaps, one of the greatest quotes of all time from the movie *The Big Lebowski* captures this point best: "Sometimes you eat the bear, and sometimes the bear eats you." It highlights the realization that sometimes you win, and sometimes you lose. Victories are hard to come by, and they should be celebrated and appreciated when you are fortunate enough to get them. Therefore, enjoy the journey, not just the ending destination. Take time to smell the roses. Don't just celebrate when you get to the finish line, instead celebrate all along the way.

When we play the game of life or chess, you enhance your enjoyment when you:

Trust the process.

Don't sweat the small stuff.

Find the positive.

Reward yourself constantly.

Grow through your experiences.

Appreciate and cherish the relationships you form.

Relish your memories.

Trust the Process

This book represents the beginning of the process. The journey may get lonely and arduous, but never stop believing in yourself, your purpose, and the process. There may be obstacles and setbacks. You may be detoured, but never be deterred. Don't you ever give up.

Mathew 17:20 says, "If you have faith as small as a mustard seed, you can say to this mountain, 'Move from here to there,' and it will move. Nothing will be impossible for you."

You will look back and marvel at the progress you've made and the obstacles you have overcome.

Don't Sweat the Small Stuff

Since we know that adversity will always come, we need to do our best not to be overwhelmed by it.

Just like the author Rich Carlson says: "Don't sweat the small stuff… and it's all small stuff."

People who enjoy life don't just live better; they may also live longer. When you enjoy things, you'll be happy and in a good mood more frequently. Scientific research has shown that physical and psychological health are closely intertwined, and positive emotions may play a positive role in preventing and managing disease. The happier you are, the less stressed you are.

Some stress can have a positive effect on us and is called good stress, or what psychologists refer to as *eustress*, the type of stress we feel when excited. Our pulse quickens, and our hormones surge, but there is no threat or fear. We feel this type of stress when we ride a roller coaster, take an exam, compete in a game

of chess, or go on a first date. This good stress keeps us feeling alive and excited about life.

Chronic stress, on the other hand, is not good. A prolonged and constant feeling of stress can negatively affect your health if it goes untreated. It can cause aches and pains, decreased energy, and causes difficulty sleeping, frequent illnesses and infections, headaches, acne, depression, diabetes, heart disease, high blood pressure, ulcers, and even weight changes.

So as Bobby McFerrin's song goes, "Don't worry, be happy."

Find the Positive

There is a common idiom about being a glass-half-full person, not a glass-half-empty person. Both people are experiencing the same situation, but one sees the glass as half full, and the other sees the glass as half empty.

Are you going to dwell on the positive (optimism) or dwell on the negative (pessimism)? While it's important to grasp the reality of your situation, you'll hold yourself back from moving

forward if you view everything in a negative way. Rather than focusing on the bad parts, it's critical to develop an optimistic mindset and positive outlook in order to optimize your ability to adapt.

Psychologists say that optimists can cope with setbacks more effectively in part, due to their ability to selectively pay attention to the positives of each situation. This phenomenon is described as attentional bias in which a person tends to focus more on the positive aspects of a bad situation rather than feeding into the negatives. If you do this, you can turn your negative experience into an opportunity for future growth.

Some examples of this are:

While I have been on ten interviews and have yet to get a job, they have prepared me for the eleventh.

I didn't lose five games. I got five opportunities to learn and get better.

Even though she couldn't visit her friends because of the pandemic, she was happy she got to spend more quality time with her husband.

My football game was canceled due to inclement weather. Instead of being upset about it, I enjoyed having the day off.

Tony, who became paralyzed from the waist down, doesn't imagine all the things he can no longer do. Instead, he is happy he still has the use of his hands and can continue to do many other things.

In addition to giving you an adaptable mindset, positivity also makes you happier. As stated earlier, scientific research has shown that physical and psychological health are closely intertwined and that positive emotions may play a positive role in preventing and managing disease. Remember, the happier you are, the less stressed you are.

Reward Yourself Constantly

Matthew 25:13 states, "Therefore keep watch, because you do not know the day or the hour."

If today could be your last day or your last game, then you have to enjoy it. Don't get so caught up in the fight that you lose sight of your victories. Reward yourself constantly. You don't have to wait to reach

your destination or goals or objectives, you should reward yourself for achieving small victories. By rewarding yourself continuously, your brain will start to link pleasure to accomplishing the task or objective and move towards it in the future. You will find yourself being more productive, effective, and generally happier. As stated earlier, the happier you are, the less stressed you are.

Rewards don't have to be anything extravagant or big. They can serve as simple, small, welcomed breaks. It needs to be proportionate to success. Don't buy yourself a car for taking out the trash; you could instead watch your favorite show, play a video game, go for a nice walk, or eat a bowl of ice cream.

It also shouldn't take you out of your productive zone, the time and environment where you get the most accomplished. You should have fun, but not too much fun. You want to reward yourself for a reasonable time frame and amount. So have one bowl of ice cream, not a gallon. A couple of hours on the video game is still okay, but don't spend the whole day on it.

Grow Through Your Experiences

Don't just go through it; grow through it. Grow through your experiences, and always strive to be better than you were yesterday. Realize failure fuels success. If you learn something, you can gain wisdom from it when used at the right time, place, or manner. Then it was not a waste of time, nor was it a waste of effort. Whether you get the idea the first time, or it takes you a little longer to catch on, as long as you learned, it isn't a waste.

Sculptor Auguste Rodin captured this point when he said, "Nothing is a waste of time if you use the experience wisely."

When we don't learn from our experiences, we can drive ourselves insane. As Einstein noted, "Insanity is doing the same thing over and over again and expecting different results."

Appreciate the Relationships You Form

Life and chess are not solitary endeavors. You are going to meet some interesting people along the way, and they are going to be part of your story.

Learn from them and appreciate them. You can learn what to do as well as what not to do. If you appreciate your relationships, you will value them. If you value them, then you will follow the golden rule and the law of attraction.

The golden rule ultimately inspires us to treat others with respect, kindness, and fairness if we want it in return. This is another example of the law of attraction. When we combine the law of attraction and the golden rule, we unleash a power unimaginable to our everyday consciousness. If you want respect, kindness, and fairness, then be more respectful, kind, and fair.

Cherish Your Memories

One of the experiences that shaped my life was the time I spent with my great grandmother. She was a victim of Alzheimer's. It was painful to watch as she lost her memory more every day. By the end she was a shell of herself and couldn't even remember her name.

This seems like the worst death. It's like your whole life didn't exist. Because I know how valuable

memories are, I try to cherish them every day. The experiences, the accomplishments, and the failures all shaped who I am today. I wouldn't trade them for anything in the world.

One way to recall and reminisce in your memories is through photographs. My wife is the photo queen. She has pictures of when we first met, every one of our children's births, birthday parties, every holiday, and so much more.

I never knew how important photos were until I met her. They are important because they communicate and document moments in time. Photos can be treasured forever because they freeze that moment in time. They help us understand and teach history. They tell a story, build connections, and evoke emotions. They can even be inspiring.

I implore you to take pictures throughout your journey in life and chess. You will be glad you did. That way, no one will ever be able to take those moments away from you.

I'd like to leave you with three thoughts. Find your spark, do no harm, and dare to care.

Every fire starts with a spark. Find yours. Find the thing that excites you and gets you up every morning, and be on fire for it.

We owe it the universe to leave it better than we found it. The least we can do is to do no harm to it or others.

And remember, every man, woman, or child can be a mentor and help others. There is only one quality necessary to be a mentor—just care.

So, I encourage you to get out there and play the game. And if you follow all the advice given to you in this book, you will checkmate life and your opponent simultaneously!